DEVELOPING YOUR
CHILD FOR

BY KENNETH A. LANE, O.D.

ILLUSTRATION & ARTWORK BY LESLIE YOUNG

LEARNING POTENTIALS PUBLISHERS, INC.

LEWISVILLE, TEXAS, USA

Dedicated to my wife Janet
for her love, patience and support.

ACKNOWLEDGEMENTS

This book would never have been completed without the help of these individuals:

Special thanks to Bob Williams and Vision Extension, Inc. for letting me use and revise activities from my first book "Reversal Errors: Theories and Therapy Procedures."

To Leslie Young for her much needed advice and talented artwork on the cover and illustrations.

To Tina Blakely for her many hours in front of the computer organizing and putting this book together.

To my vision therapists, Cheryl Ablon, Susan Oliver, Elita Lee, Sherron Garrison, Donna Latson, and Debbie Paget for their input and advice on the activities.

To my secretaries, Tina Blakely and Carol White, for their many hours in typing these pages.

To Debbie Paget and Cheryl Close for proofreading this book.

Special appreciation to the many children and parents who have used and worked with these activities. This book would not have been possible without them.

FOREWORD

---

*   *   *

"Dr. Lane's book is a much needed book, both for parents and teachers alike.

Too often today, many people hold the view that vision has little or no relationship to a child's achievement or general behavior. There are even different beliefs in the visual care profession, which must be confusing to the public. This is especially true for parents who have received contradictory opinions and diagnoses from different specialists. Parents often have to decide what to do about their child's vision without the background and education necessary to grasp a true picture.

Dr. Lane's new edition, with a helpful introduction and following chapter activities, helps parents to see that vision and visual abilities are a part of total human functioning. His premise that vision is a very important element in the way a child develops, learns and achieves in school is a belief that we hold here at the National Institute of Child Development, Inc..

The theoretical and background information given in Dr. Lane's book will provide knowledge that will help in practical decisions about a child's vision. His concern with vision, visual abilities and visual performance, and how these can be made more efficient and developmentally utilized is very reassuring.

In today's climate of life in which we dehumanize just about every experience a child encounters, it is refreshing to find Dr. Lane's book describing how parents need not stop short with just an eye examination for their children. The book gives clear evidence that parents do not have to allow their children's future to be shortchanged just because they passed their last eye examination, nor do they have to wait for help. This book gives clear advice about making vision a more effective two-way system -- the <u>motor</u> and <u>functional</u> aspects of seeing. It also explains, that once this two-way strategy becomes coordinated and attuned to the sensory system, children become active participants in the modification of their behavior. This seems only natural in a society that is concerned with prevention, and in ways to help children avoid early school failure."

Clyde Gillespie, Director
National Institute of Child Development

*   *   *

"As I thumbed through Developing Your Child For Success, noting the hundreds of tasks that are spelled out in detail -- with materials either provided or easily made by teachers or parents, I was struck with several competing reactions. As a clinical psychologist with a practice centering around neuropsychological assessment, frequently with children with developmental or traumatically acquired learning impairments, I first pictured the faces of the parents I had been forced to tell about their child's impairment. The first thing they want to know is what they can do to help ameliorate the problem; special schools, placement in special education, private tutors, and time-consuming methods -- most completely unsupported by medical insurance -- were anything but satisfactory as an answer. With this book, Dr. Lane and his staff have provided at least a partial answer, a straightforward set of procedures, carefully constructed through years of experience, with the ultimate purpose of providing a method of systematically engendering a cautious hopefulness and a sense of efficacy in parents or teachers.

This work is much needed and welcomed, and I shall look forward to utilizing and testing it with my clients. It is a treasury of tradecraft in developmental optometry and, perhaps, in related fields of endeavor as well."

Steven E. Greer, P.h. D.
Clinical Psychologist

*   *   *

PREFACE

My years of working with young school-aged children have shown me that many children who are experiencing difficulty in their early school years can be helped, especially if help is given at an early age. Young children who are reversing letters and numbers, who have poor printing skills, and are having difficulty learning to read are often immature in the basic perceptual and motor skills needed to do these tasks. Waiting and hoping that they will outgrow these problems is not advisable. Many children never totally overcome these problems. Many take years to learn how to compensate for them. Meanwhile, the feelings of failure and low self-esteem that are developed in these early years can carry over and affect their adult lives.

This book is designed so that parents can help their children avoid early school failure. It is not designed to replace a professional evaluation. Nor does this book teach children to read. Teachers teach children to read. This book, however, gives a child the skills that make it easier for him/her to be taught. It enables parents to actively participate in their child's development.

Throughout the book I use the pronouns "he" and "him" to denote children. This is not intended to discriminate against females or to insinuate that only males need help in these areas. This is used solely for simplicity in the grammatical construction of the text.

I urge parents who feel that their child may have a learning problem to seek professional help. Many professionals including: Developmental Optometrists, Occupational Therapists, Psychologists, Speech Pathologists and Special Educators can assist parents and offer programs that are designed to help children with learning related problems.

There is nothing more disheartening than seeing a once happy child dejected and defeated by the time he/she is in third grade. By giving their children the skills necessary for success, parents may never have to watch their children experience the frustration associated with early school failure.

TABLE OF CONTENTS

INTRODUCTION

Most adults do not remember their early reading experiences. Reading for them is now an effortless automatic process. However, for many children it is a nightmare. There are between five and ten million children who suffer from some type of learning disability. That is between 2% and 20% of our total school population.[1] If you include all the children who have some level of learning problem that has not been diagnosed or recognized, then that percentage would be much higher.

Why is it that so many children today have difficulty learning to read and can't keep up with the rest of the class? I think we have to realize that the school pressures and work expected of children today is much more than it was when their parents went to school. Reading and succeeding in school are becoming more important in our society. We expect more out of each generation and for good reason. Society in general reads more and places a higher importance on reading than in the past. At the turn of the century, 35,000 books were published world wide every year. Now over 400,000 books are published yearly. At the turn of the century, more people were in agriculture than any other profession. Now there are more people teaching in universities than are in agriculture.[2]

Many children are not mature enough in their basic perceptual and motor development to keep up with the enormous amount of school work that is expected of them. Just because a child is six years old chronologically, doesn't mean that his/her motor and perceptual skills are also at a six year old level. While it is the job of the preschool and kindergarten teacher to identify a child she feels is not keeping up with the other children, it is also the parents' responsibility to have their child evaluated if they feel there is a problem. Most perceptual learning occurs from age 4 1/2 to 7 1/2[3] and most neurological development is completed by the age of 10.[4] The earlier a child is identified as having potential learning problems, the easier it is to help him/her.

While the following signs and symptoms do not automatically mean that a child has a learning disability, children who have these symptoms seem to have a higher probability of having school problems.

1

1. Delayed speech or motor development. Most children speak their first word and walk by 12 to 13 months[5]. If a child was slow learning to walk or talk or had to receive speech therapy, it may also indicate delayed perceptual -motor development.

2. Hereditary. 50% of learning disabilities run in the family. If a parent had a lot of difficulty in school, there is a good chance his/her children may also have problems.

3. Poor gross motor skills. These children tend to be clumsy. They often have poor balance skills. For example, they may have had a lot of difficulty learning to ride their bikes. Most children should be able to stand and balance on one leg for ten seconds by the age of 5 1/2[6].

4. Poor fine motor skills. These children are usually poor at copying designs and have poor printing skills. When they get in school, they lose their place easily when they read or use their finger as a marker when they read. They also make numerous errors and are slow copying off the blackboard. By age 5 1/2, most children should be able to copy a triangle and by age 7, a vertical diamond[7].

5. Birth complications or premature birth. Children with a birth weight under five pounds have a higher probability of learning problems.

6. Difficulty remembering their right and left. Between the ages of six and seven years, the child's sense of right and left appears[8]. Between seven and nine, the child can recognize right and left not only in himself/herself, but also in a person facing him/her.

7. Reversing letters and numbers. All young children will reverse some letters and numbers. Children need a mental age of 6 1/2 to overcome left-right reversals.[9] If a child is still reversing at age 7, this may indicate a problem.

Reading is an extremely complex neurological process. It is even more complex than learning to talk. When you think about it, we are given years to learn how to talk but only months to learn how to read.[10] By the age of six, we are expected to learn how to read whether we are neurologically mature enough or not. In Chapter One, I will explain the complex processes involved in reading. The purpose of this chapter is not to impress you with terminology but to stress to you how complex reading is. To be a successful reader, a young child needs to be both emotionally and perceptually developed.

CHAPTER ONE

UNDERSTANDING THE MANY FACTORS INVOLVED IN READING

Reading is not a continuous process. The visual input is presented as chunks or packages which are re-assembled in the brain and appear to be one continuous visual image. The eye moves across the page taking in visual information. The actual movements of the eye are called saccadic eye movements and the pauses to take in and process visual information are called fixations. If the eye has to reread, this is called a regression. We know that saccadic eye movements take about 10% of the reading time and regressions about 15%. This means that most of our reading time is spent in fixations.[11]

While the eye pauses during each fixation, the brain can pick up visual information as far as 14 letter positions to the right of the fixation point. The fixation point is the letter your eye looks at in a word. The brain can recognize the length of a word 13 to 14 positions to the right of fixation, the visual shape of a word 10 to 12 positions to the right of fixation, but can only identify letters and words 4 to 6 positions to the right of fixation. This small area where letter and word identification occurs is called the span of recognition.[12] It is not until the sixth grade that readers read more than a single word in the average span of recognition. In other words, it takes until the sixth grade for even good readers to identify more than a single word each time their eyes pause as they read across the line of print.

How far does the brain know to move the eyes for each movement? It seems that the brain makes anticipatory plans based on contextual and peripheral visual information and then moves the eyes to informative areas of the text. The average length of movement (saccadic fixation) is 8 to 10 letter positions [13] and the optimal viewing position (the location in the word where the eye pauses) is usually on a letter near the front of the word.[14] The brain uses peripheral visual information and information derived from the reader's understanding of the text to anticipate what is coming. It then moves the eyes to the area of the text that it feels will give the reader the most information.

During the actual eye movement across the page (saccadic fixation), the threshold for detecting visual information is raised so that no visual information is processed. This is called saccadic suppression.[15] If the brain did not do this, we would see a blurred image as we moved our eyes from fixation point to fixation point. When the eye pauses for the fixation, the meaning of the word is accessed. During the first 25% of the fixation, the brain decides where it will move the eye the next time and for the remaining 75%, actual word identification occurs.[16] The start of the saccadic eye movement activates what are called transient channels. These channels discontinue the sustained activity which has been used to process the visual information during the fixation.[17] If the brain did not do this, we would have what is called visual persistence. This would be like an after image as visual information from the last fixation would interfere with the visual information being processed by the new fixation. Therefore, not only does the brain suppress visual information as it moves across the page but also the visual processing from the last fixation. Actual cognitive processing in the brain continues but not processing of visual information. The brain continues to digest what it already has stored but blocks out old visual information so it doesn't interfere with new visual information.

There seems to be fast and slow processes that take place in normal reading. Both types start as soon as the word is presented, but the slow processes do not begin to affect word processing until about 200 msec after the word is presented. For good readers, the fast processes produce enough information to permit the reader to ignore or abort the results from the slow processes.[18] The slow processes demand maximum information hence maximum use of visual acuity. They depend on accurate recognition of letters and letter sequences rather than less accurate sources such as peripheral visual information. Whenever accuracy is demanded, or when the material is difficult, the slow processes dominate word recognition. If the reader can get by with information available to the fast processes, he will not have to use the slow processes which require accurate letter identification. Good readers mainly use the fast processes. For example, by using information available in their peripheral vision and semantic, syntaxic, and context clues, accurate individual letter identification is not necessary. They can guess what is coming next and thereby be helped in identifying the word they are looking at without identifying each letter in the word.

Syntax is the knowledge of grammar and word associations to make sense of a sentence. By knowing the rules of grammar, a good reader can make predictions of what word may follow.[19] For example, pronouns (I, you, he, she, it, etc.) usually begin a noun phrase. Prepositions (to, at, in) begin a prepositional phrase. If we had a sentence, "The little boy ran home", we can predict what class of word is left out. The _____ boy ran home (the word left out must be an adjective). The little ____ ran home (the word left out must be a noun).

Semantics is the knowledge of word meaning.[20] Consider the word "visit". Visit requires an animate, mobile subject. Trees, while animate, cannot move of their own volition, so the phrase "the tree visited" does not occur. Visit also requires an object whose referent is either a person or a place. We visit someone or somewhere. We know that the word that follows "visit" will be either a person or a place.

Context clues mean being familiar with a topic. If we are reading about pirates, the story probably includes ships, treasure, etc. and we expect to see words about these things. If we are reading about baseball and we read the sentence, "Babe Ruth hit a home ___", we know the word is probably "run".

Readers, therefore, move their eyes across the page and pause to take in visual information. Knowledge of syntax, context and semantics help the reader anticipate what is coming next. This information plus information on word length and shape from our peripheral vision help the brain to decide where to move the eyes next.

Each area of the text is looked at several times, initially by our peripheral vision, then by the area near our central vision, then by the central vision, and last by the area near our central vision to the left of fixation point. The overlapping fields of view promote a perceptual integration of the whole line of print in the same way that integrating all the views of a picture can lead to a constructed picture. This gives us the impression that we are looking at a large part of a line of print when we are really only looking at not much more than one word at a time.

You are now familiar with how the brain moves our eyes as we read and what information helps in these decisions but what happens during the fixation when actual visual processing and letter and word identification occurs?

As our eyes pause to read, the brain will screen the letters in the word to identify them. About 20 features (such as vertical line, horizontal lines, etc.) are used to differentiate among the 75 characters we use in reading and math. The characters are 26 uppercase letters, 26 lowercase letters, the numbers 0-9, and standard punctuation marks.[21] Usually good readers only need one or two features to identify a letter. The important thing to understand is that we do not process letters and words like we do pictures. Pictures seem to be stored in the brain in pictorial forms, however, letters and words appear to be taken out of visual form and changed to an abstract written code.[22, 23] The letter "T", for example, may be coded as a horizontal line on top of a vertical line. The letter "b" may be coded as a vertical line and a loop on the right lower side. Therefore, anytime the brain scans a figure with a horizontal line on top of a vertical line, it will interpret this as a "T". This is why we can read handwriting we have never seen. If the brain stored letters and words in pictural form, we would be unable to recognize unfamiliar print or handwriting, unless the print or handwriting style was already stored in our memory. We also know that letters could not be processed in pictorial form when you consider that 98% of the optic pathway from the eye to the visual centers of the brain can be removed and we can still discriminate different patterns.[24] This concept is important when we consider certain reversal errors in young children. We know that the standard scanning patterns of letters appears to be from top to bottom and from left to right. (By scan pattern, I mean the visual scanning of the letter one part at a time.) If, however, a young child's attention is first attracted to a point of a letter which attracts his attention first (salient feature), letters such as "b" and "d" may be confused.[25] For example, the proper scan pattern for a "b" could be vertical line, loop, however, if the child started to scan from the loop in both "b" and "d", the brain would get the same code; loop, vertical line. Hence "b's" and "d's" would be confused as they appear to be identical due to the same code.

As we mentioned earlier, letters and words are identified by our central, not our peripheral vision. The area of the eye which has most of the feature detectors for letter identification is in a small part of the retina called the fovea. This small area is only about 1.5 mm in diameter.[26] The fovea has all the cones for sharp visual acuity. The peripheral retina has the rods which we use for night vision. The visual image must fall in the fovea for letter identification to occur. For example, if we are directly fixating a letter, that letter is being sampled by something like a grid of 30x30 feature detectors, two letters further out in our peripheral vision a letter is being sampled by a 19x19 grid of feature detectors and two letters further out by a grid of 15x15 feature detectors. Because the brain does not have enough feature detectors, we cannot identify letters more than 4 to 6 positions from the point of fixation. Letters will compete for the available feature detectors. This is called "crowding".[27] Because of this crowding problem, the brain scans areas of letters and words that give it the most useful information. It simply can't process all the information available to it. We know that the tops of letters[28] and the beginning of words supply the most useful information. This is why the eye usually fixates on a letter near the front of a word. Not only does the brain scan individual letters and change the visual image to a code, but it also records the letter's orientation and position in the word. In fact, we know that letter orientation and position are processed in different brain channels than the channels used to identify the different features in letters for letter identification.[29, 30]

While letters compete with each other for feature detectors, good readers are able to use their knowledge of spelling patterns (orthography) to help in letter identification. In the English language, letters occur in certain positions in words more frequently than in other positions.[31] For example, in the pseudo-word "hortey" all the letters are in positions they are normally in for a six letter English word. In the pseudo-word "yterho" all the letters are not in position they are normally in for a six letter word.[32] As you can see, hortey is much easier to pronounce and remember than yterho. By being in positions they are normally in, the letters help to identify each other just as words help to identify each other in sentences because they are in positions they are normally in. Good readers use this knowledge for letter identification when they don't have enough feature detectors for normal identification.

Reading requires a multitude of skills. Not only must the brain move the eyes to the proper location, but the visual image must focus on the fovea. The letter's visual features, orientation and position in the word must be interpreted and coded. This information plus knowledge of orthography, syntax, semantics, context and peripheral visual clues are all used to help identify the word. Adult readers have the luxury of using all of this information when they read. Young readers, however, do not. Consider the fact that a good reader in first grade only looks at about 30% of a word for each fixation[33] That is not much more than one or two letters at a time. This indicates that young children spend most of their reading time decoding individual letters and letter groups to form words. Basic perceptual skills are absolutely necessary for the young child to succeed in reading. To break down the visual image and code the individual letters, the child must have a thorough understanding of such basic perceptual prerequisites as feature identification, letter orientation, and proper sequencing. They must also have the visual skills necessary for proper focusing on the individual letters and the fine motor skills necessary for proper and accurate eye movements. The activities in this book are designed to develop these skills. Chapter Two will explain the visual and motor abilities necessary to develop the perceptual skills required for reading.

CHAPTER TWO

DEVELOPING THE PERCEPTUAL SKILLS NEEDED FOR READING

Perceptual-Motor Development

We are not born with the complex perceptual skills needed for reading. These skills are developed through the child's early childhood experiences. The ability to understand the component parts of letters and proper orientation of letters is learned. To be able to move your eyes efficiently and effortlessly and aim them where you want to is developed through trial and error. The child comes into this world with very few perceptual skills. In six years they must be developed to the point that the child can master the most complex neurological processes he will ever have to master - learning to read.

For years many people felt that the world a young infant first sees is nothing but a mass of shapeless blobs.[34] After all, if the infant has never touched or had any physical contact with objects in the real world, would he be able to know where one object started and another one ended? Does everything he sees appear to run together like shapeless blobs of different colors?

We now have a little better idea of what a young infant sees. His ability to see detailed features of anything very far from him is very poor. A child of one month has visual acuities of between 20/400 to 20/1200.[35] This means that he sees at 20 feet what you and I can see at 400 to 1200 feet. However, by six months old, his vision has already improved to between 20/50 to 20/200. When something is near to him, the infant does respond to information dealing with depth and motion. In other words, he can perceive distance and notices motion. These skills appear to be innate.

Very young infants are not affected by feature differences. For them, movement is predominant. They respond to a change in motion but not to a change in size, shape, or color. They do not seem to respond to stationary objects. As early as two weeks, an infant shows fear of approaching objects

9

but not objects moving away.[36] The infant is not sensitive to information that is stationary or a 2-D form. By eight weeks, he can notice different colors and has some degree of form perception (notices that one ojbect is different from another). He is capable of discriminating among different orientations of the same shape (orientation discrimination), can tell it is the same object even though it appears to get smaller the farther it is from him (size consistency), and can even tell when an object is partially hidden by another that it is a complete object even though he can't see the whole thing (completion).[37] It seems therefore, that rather than living in a world of shapeless blobs, the infant is born with some basic perceptual skills. We know, however, that these skills must be developed. Experiments with animals raised in the dark for a short period of time showed that these animals had more difficulty with form perception than normally raised animals.[38] Therefore, even though some perception is innate, it is very crude and must be developed.

What is perception? Perception is identifying and understanding our environment. Vision perception is understanding what we see. Auditory perception is understanding what we hear. Tactile perception is understanding what we feel. It is the combination of all of them that gives us "perception." A child develops perception through experiences with his environment. Each perceptual area develops with the help of the other areas. When we see an object, we also have an idea how it feels, smells, or even tastes. When we hear a sound, we can visualize what the object looks like that made the sound. A child does not develop visual perception with his eyes alone, nor does he see with just one part of his brain. Meaningful vision is produced only by integrated action among many parts of the brain including, in addition to visual stimuli, sensory stimuli from our muscles, touch and our balance systems.[39] Perception develops as the child develops, with the maximum development between 4 to 7 1/2 years old.[40] A child whose vision and motor skills develop normally usually has normal visual perceptual development and is ready for the complex processes needed for reading. Children who are immature in these skills often experience frustration in learning to read.

Children develop in a normal developmental sequence. Even before birth, the child is developing skills. As early as the fifth gestational month, eye movements are produced by vestibular influences.[41] The child's ability to look at an object, focus, and align his eyes together develops at the end of the second and third postnatal month.[42] By five months, a child's eyes will follow a slowly moving object. When a baby of six months hears a noise, he is capable of directing his eyes and head in order to see the object. When he sees it, he tries to grasp it in order to take it to his mouth. By eight months, he sits independently and creeps on hands and knees and by 12 months, stands up.[43] The first year of crawling, standing up, and walking permits the development of new interaction of perceptual modalities which permit him to discover the surrounding sphere. During the second year, the action of gravitational forces produces reinforcement and development of body schemes through experimental walking, falling, and brushing objects. At this stage, a child also

10

develops body awareness and develops knowledge of his own body and body parts. During the third and fourth years of development, the child has the ability to do a skilled movement with one side of the body while the other side is doing another movement. By the fifth and sixth year, the child has established a preference in using one side of the body over the other.[44] Neurological organization is virtually completed within the first decade of life.[45] This is why it is extremely important that a child who has immature perceptual-motor skills be identified and given help early.

In order to understand how motor activity and motor development are essential for learning, you need to have some understanding of brain development.

Since creation, the evolutional trend in brain development has been to transfer control of an activity from lower brain areas to higher brain areas. As the nervous system evolved to meet the expanding needs of existence, the newer structures tended to duplicate older structures and functions and improve upon them rather than to devise different functions. Thus, the same kinds of function are repeated at several levels of the brain. The higher levels as they developed also remained dependent upon the lower structures. The cerebral cortex, which is where our higher cognitive skills such as reading occur, would not be able to interpret sensations that carry information from the environment if it were not for the transmission and processing of the lower brain areas such as the vestibular system, brain stem, and cerebellum. A child thinks with his whole brain, not just the higher brain areas. The educators' error has been in the thinking that all perception and cognitive skills are exclusively cortical (meaning pertaining only to higher brain areas). Thus, overlooking the probability that some lower brain functions may also still be critical for these skills.[46]

The older and more primitive areas of the brain are concerned with primitive functions that are critical for the survival of the species. These functions include not only regulating our breathing and emotions but controlling our posture and basic motor skills that are necessary for survival.

The vestibular system controls our posture, equilibrium, and spatial orientation. It consists of the utricle, saccule, and semicircular canals of the inner ear. This apparatus specifically responds to gravitational forces and accelerated or retarded movement.[47]

The cerebellum is the part of the brain that controls motor output. It acts like a computer and takes sensory input and controls motor output. It works with the vestibular system and controls our balance and keeps our head and eyes stabilized against body movement. It coordinates the muscles that control our eye movements to keep our eyes on what we are looking at. The body below the neck is merely a platform for the brain and the eyes are the windows to the brain. If the platform is out of balance, the computing mechanisms of the brain which are predominately visual will also be out of balance. Children who have inefficient cerebellum-vestibular skills usually have very poor balance skills. They also have poor eye movements and lose their place easily when they read. These children also have very poor handwriting skills.[48]

The brain stem is a very primitive part of the brain. This part of the brain controls our central nervous system. It organizes sensory information and promotes general alertness. Disorders, such as hyperactivity and distractability, are often associated with this area of the brain. Also, motor patterns of the eyes and of the total trunk and extremities working together may be organized and mediated in the brain stem.[49]

The purpose of stating these facts is to stress the point that the parts of the brain that evolved first are concerned with basic functions such as posture, eye movements, motor output and balance. The newer parts of the brain (the higher brain areas - the cortex) are also concerned with these functions but are also concerned with new functions such as language and reading. If you understand that each developmental step is dependent upon a certain degree of maturation of the previous steps,[50] you will see that reading and language are dependent upon proper development of the lower brain areas. As I stated before, the child reads with his whole brain.

The whole brain is concerned with the basic functions of motor and postural control. In order for the cortex to function properly and use most of its resources for higher brain functions such as reading, it transfers many of its motoric responsibilities to automatic levels.[51] As intentional or voluntary motor activities become self-governed, the higher cortical levels can be used for other learning processes which may or may not be involved with motor activities themselves. The more the intentional or coordinated motor activities can be reproduced automatically in a satisfactory way, the greater the possibility for learning. This is the principle of "Corporal Potentiality."[52] If the brain can leave the more basic primitive functions to be handled by the lower brain areas and not have to have the higher brain areas help out, then the higher brain areas can use all their energy for their functions and learning is possible. Jackson's Law states that "In the case of damage to the central nervous system, functions which appear latest in evolution are lost first."[53] This means that in the case of a head injury, the brain will protect its more primitive functions first, due to survival considerations at the expense of newer functions such as reading and language. Since reading is fairly new on the evolutionary scale, it is not considered as important as other functions.

The famous psychologist, Piaget, believed that motor experiences are the foundation of mental development[54] and that all cognitive mechanisms are based on motor activity. At the beginning of life, motor activity develops before mental actions, then both work together and coexist, and then finally, mental action subordinates motor activity. The premise here is that proper development of motor skills is critical for learning. For a child to have the eye movement skills necessary to keep his eyes on the proper letters in a word

12

when he reads and to be able to have the eye hand coordination skills necessary to write, his motor skills must be developed to the point of being automatic. This usually comes with normal development. The child, as he matures, develops proper balance and gross motor skills. By gross motor, I mean large muscles such as those used for walking and standing. Development then proceeds from gross to fine motor. The large muscle groups lying toward the center of the body precede development of the small muscle groups lying at the extremity. Thus total arm precedes elbow, which precedes the wrist, which precedes the fingers and so forth.[55] This is why we see so many children with learning disabilities who are uncoordinated and have poor balance and motor skills. Many of the activities in this book are designed to train motor skills. Not only gross motor, but also fine motor skills such as visual-motor (eye-hand coordination) and ocular-motor (eye movement) skills. By having the child use his whole body and move through space, we are training the whole brain. If we just let him sit in front of a computer or try and teach his "left" and "right" by clues in his shoes or on his wrists, we are using mainly the higher brain areas. However, if we let the child experience directions and the sides of his body through balance and motor activities that involve the whole body, then we are training the whole brain including the lower levels.

Vision

While motor skills are stressed in this book, they are not the only skills necessary for good reading skills. Vision also plays a large role. Scientists estimate that three billion on and off impulses flow into the central nervous system per second.[56] Of these, two billion come from the eyes, a billion from each eye per second. Good visual skills are, therefore, critical for good reading skills.

As we mentioned earlier, letters and words are identified by our central vision. The area of the eye which has most of the feature detectors for letter identification is a small part of the retina called the fovea. This area is only about 1.5 mm in diameter. The image we are looking at must fall on this area for letter identification. If the image is blurred due to poor focusing skills or poor eye sight or if the child does not aim his eyes accurately as a result of poor eye movements (ocular motor), then decoding for identification will be hindered.

Poor ocular motor skills are usually caused by immature gross motor and balance skills. As I mentioned earlier, the cerebellum-vestibular system controls our balance and eye tracking skills. It allows our eyes to be aimed where we want regardless of our head and body movement. Since even good readers do not look at much more than one word each time they move their eyes across a page to read, poor eye control can cause a scrambling effect and confusion by causing words to overlap and run together. Consider the fact that a young reader just learning to read is decoding not much more than one letter at a time and you can see the visual confusion that can be caused by poor ocular motor skills.

As I stated earlier, the more primitive functions that are critical for survivial purposes have a higher priority to the brain than the newer language and reading functions. Clear and single vision are basic for survival. Blurred vision or double vision is not tolerated by the brain. All of its resources will be used to make sure we have clear vision and that we do not see double. If a child has a problem using his two eyes together or if he has to struggle to keep his print clear when he reads, higher brain processing will be affected. The energy and resources that could have been used for processing reading material will be used to keep the print clear and the eyes lined up properly. The child's reading skills will suffer.

Vision is much more than seeing the 20/20 line on the eye chart. Vision also includes the child's focusing, ocular motor and eye teaming skills. All of these areas must be working smoothly and efficiently for reading processing to occur without interference. Vision problems associated with reading include:

1.) losing your place easily when moving your gaze from desk work to chalkboard or when copying from the text to notebook.

2.) making errors in copying from the chalkboard to paper on the desk.

3.) using a marker or finger to keep your place while reading.

4.) losing your place often during reading.

5.) mistaking words with the same or similar beginnings.

6.) whispering to self for reinforcement while reading silently.

7.) misaligning digits in columns of numbers.

8.) headaches after reading or near work.

9.) burning or itching eyes after doing near vision work.

10.) holding the book too close to your face.

11.) blinking excessively when doing near work, but not otherwise.

12.) rubbing your eyes during or after short periods of reading.

13.) complaining of seeing double during reading.

14.) closing or covering one eye when reading or writing.

15.) having your comprehension decline as reading continues.

Sequential Verses Simultaneous Processing

The ability to process information and to solve a particular problem usually relies on one of two processing systems. If we have all the information available to us at one time and if we can continually analyze all the details of the information, this is called simultaneous processing.[57]   Children who have problems in simultaneous processing usually have poor reading comprehension skills. They have a difficult time in understanding the semantic relationships among the many separate linguistic elements in a sentence or story. They cannot integrate many details at once. It may be first noticed in young children when they continually leave out parts of geometric shapes or pictures they are trying to copy.

If we are given information a little bit at a time and we are not able to continually analyze all the details of the information, this is called sequential processing.[58]   Children who have problems in sequential processing have a difficult time remembering things in sequence. For example, they have difficulty remembering verbal instructions, the letters in the alphabet or the days of the week. This will affect their school work in that they will have problems in remembering spelling words, math rules, and how to sound out words (phonics).

In reality, children usually use a combination of sequential and simultaneous processing to learn and solve problems. However, with some children, one of these processes functions better than the other. These children then have a preferred learning style. If this is the case, he should be taught in school using his preferred style and spend extra time working to improve the other.

Laterality - Directionality

The young infant who grasps a toy and puts it in his mouth, the young child who is playing on the swings, and the child who is building a house with his blocks are all experiencing perceptual-motor development. Through active movement, the child is gathering information on himself and the external world. This information is the building block for the perceptual skills needed for reading and succeeding in schoool. By mentally reflecting on these different physical experiences, the child begins to develop not only concepts about specific attributes of each object (such as round, smooth, heavy, etc.) but he also begins to develop the underlying concepts necessary for logical thinking. For example, understanding addition and subtraction requires several developmental prerequisites such as understanding the concepts of "more", "less", and "equal to", all of which are derived from physical activity with

15

objects.[59] The perception of size, distance, position, and shape are not properties that are given by vision alone. We perceive these properties only by the integratioin of touch, pressure, and movement with vision.

While the child is learning about the physical characteristics of external objects, he is also learning about himself. Through body movement and the resulting inputs from various muscles to the brain, the child learns his own body imagery. He learns about his head, arms, and leg positions compared to other parts of his body. But most importantly, he learns where he is in space in relation to gravity. Development proceeds from a "self-reference" system to an "objective-reference" system.[60] This means that we have to have a complete understanding of our own position in space before we can understand an external object's position in space. If the child is to understand the proper orientation of letters and numbers, he must have a complete understanding of his own orientation first. There is no "right" and "left" in space. We must construct the coordinates of space by understanding our own first.

Laterality is the internal awareness of the two sides of the body and their difference.[61] It is not just knowing our "right" and "left", it is understanding our "right side" from our "left side." Laterality must be learned. It is only by experimenting with the two sides of the body and their relationship to each other that we come to distinguish between the two systems. The primary pattern out of which this differentiation develops is from balance. Balancing puts one side of the body against the other. Walking, running, and riding a bike all help to develop laterality awareness. With this help, it is easier for the child to have an understanding of his own "right" and "left" by the time he is mature enough at six years of age.

Directionality is the understanding of an external object's position in space in relationship to ourselves. It is the projection outside the child of the laterality which he has developed for himself. By having an understanding of his own "left side" and "right side", he is aware that an external figure or object also has a right and left side. Since a child cannot feel the letters when he reads, his eyes must do what his hands can't. He must visually scan the letters and understand that they have a right and left side and know that there is a difference between the two. For a child with no laterality and directionality skills, there is no proper direction for a "b" or "d." To him they are both the same.

In chapter one, I explained the complex proceses involved in reading. In this chapter, I explained the perceptual and motor skills that are needed for a child to learn to read and be successful in school. Chapter three will explain how to use the activities in this book to develop these skills.

———

CHAPTER 3

HOW TO USE THIS BOOK TO DEVELOP YOUR CHILD'S

PERCEPTUAL-MOTOR SKILLS

The activities in this book are designed to help give a child the necessary perceptual-motor skills needed to succeed in school. The activities are divided into the following eight categories:

1. Motor
2. Visual Motor
3. Ocular Motor
4. Vision
5. Laterality
6. Directionality
7. Sequential Processing
8. Simultaneous Processing

The activities in each category are not in any particular order. All of the activities are of equal importance. You do not have to start with the first activity in each category. Each activity in each category is divided into several different levels. Level 1 is the easiest and Level 5 is the most difficult. Not all the activities have all five levels. Many of the activities start at Level 2. Therefore, that would be the lowest and the easiest level for that particular activity. Some activities have a letter after a particular level. Consider these activities as being in the same level. For example, Level 3-A and 3-B are both Level 3 activities. Definitions of all the equipment used in these activities can be found in the glossary.

In order for the activities in this book to be beneficial, it is recommended that the child work on them three times a week. The suggested number of activities per session is five with the time alloted for each activity to be five to ten minutes. The length of time and number of activities can vary depending on the time available and the child's ability to attend to a task. In order for this program to be successful, the child should eventually experience all the activities in this book.

Children five and under should start with the lowest level in each activity. For children six and older, start with Level 2 in each activity. You should mix the activities in each session so that the child is not doing all of one category of activities. For example, you do not want to do only laterality activities. Always do at least one motor activity during each session. For example, for one session you might do one motor, one visual motor, one laterality, one sequential, and one ocular motor activity. If the child seems to be getting a lot of benefit from one particular activity or if you feel he needs to continue to work on that activity, continue on it the next session. However, do not do the same activity more than six sessions in a row. Make a note of a particularly beneficial activity and go back to it again at a later date. By varying the activities, you will keep the child's interest and have a more successful program.

If an activity is too difficult for the child, go down to the next lowest level. If that is also too difficult or there is no lower level, do another activity in the same category. For example, if the child is having difficulty with one sequential processing activity, try another sequential processing activity. Make a note that a particular activity was too difficult and go back to it at a later date.

If an activity is too easy, don't go to the next highest level in that activity; go on to a different activity in the same category. Always stay at a particular level in each category until all the activities are done, then go to the next highest level. For example, do all the Level 2 activities in motor before you do any Level 3 motor activities.

To summarize:

1. Do five activities per session.

2. Do at least one motor activity per session.

3. Vary the categories to get a good mix.

4. Five and under, start at the lowest level.

5. Six and older, start at Level 2.

6. If the activity is too hard, go to the next lowest level. If there is not a lower level in that particular activity, do another activity in the same category.

7. Activities that are too difficult can be repeated at a later date.

8. If the activity is too easy, go on to a different activity in the same category..

9. Stay with an activity until you feel the child has mastered it but don't do the same activity more than six sessions in a row. Make a note of beneficial activities and repeat them at a later date.

10. Do all the same level activities in a particular category before going to the next highest level.

The following is an example of what five sessions of activities might look like:

SESSION 1.

Walking rail - Level 2-A
Bean bag basketball - Level 2
Rhythm - Level 2-A
Bilateral circles - Level 2
Pencil push ups - Level 2

SESSION 2.

Walking rail - Level 2-A
Gross motor sequence - Level 2
Numbered circles on blackboard - Level 2
Pencils with numbers - Level 2
Bilateral circles - Level 2

SESSION 3.

Walking rail - Level 2-B
Bean bag basketball - Level 2
Rhythm - Level 2-A
Pencils with numbers - Level 2
Pencil push ups - Level 2

SESSION 4.

Trampoline - Level 2
Gross motor sequence - Level 2
Numbered circles on blackboard - Level 2
Pencil push ups - Level 2
Geo boards - Level 2

SESSION 5.

Trampoline - Level 2
Rhythm - Level 2-A
Pencils with numbers - Level 2
Bilateral circles - Level 2
Geo boards - Level 2

To see an example of a daily activities sheet, please refer to pages 309 & 310.

THERAPY PROCEDURES

Train a child in the way he should go,
and when he is old he will not turn from it.

Proverbs 22:6 (NIV)

SECTION I

MOTOR THERAPY PROCEDURES

Stepping Stones

Purpose: Motor

Materials: Different colored tile or carpet cut into 4" squares. Have 20 squares. 10 one color and 10 another color. Metronome

Method: The child is to walk on the squares. He is to keep his body straight and have good posture.

Level 1-A

1. Put the squares in a straight line. The child is to walk on them and keep his balance.

Level 1-B

1. Arrange the squares, slightly off center with one color on the right of center and the other on the left of center. For example,

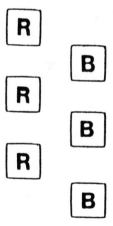

Have the child walk on the squares and call out the side that is stepping on the square. For example, each time he steps on the blue square he calls out "right" and each time he steps on the red square he calls out "left".

2. Put the squares in various patterns that make up letters or numbers. For example,

R R R R R

R

R

R

R

R

Have the child walk on the patterns and tell you which letter or number it is.

One Foot Hop

Purpose: Motor

Materials: None

Method: Have the child do the following activities.

Level 1

1. Have the child hop in place on one leg, hop four steps forward, four steps backward, hop to the left, hop to the right, hop in place and turn around.

2. Repeat with the opposite foot.

Level 2

1. Hop while grasping the ankle with the opposite hand behind the back.

2. Hop while grasping the leg in front of the body with both hands.

3. The child should try and do at least 10 hops across the room on each foot.

Heel and Toe Rock

Purpose: Motor

Materials: None

Method: Have the child do the following activities while he is standing with his feet together and his arms hanging at his side.

Level 1

1. Rise on his toes for three counts, lower his heels and lift his toes for three counts.

2. Rock back and forth holding each balance position for three counts.

3. Have him hold his balance for longer periods of time.

4. Do the same activities but have him do them with his arms folded in front of his chest.

Level 2

1. Same as level 1, but the child does the activities with his eyes closed. Only do these activities for three counts.

Bean Bag Basketball

Purpose: Motor

Materials: Bean bags, trash can, balance rail

Method: Put a trash can or bucket at various distances from the child.

Level 1

1. He is to try and throw the bean bag into the can. Have him use one hand at a time then both hands together. He can throw over or under hand.

Level 2

1. Have the child stand on the end of the walking rail in a heel to toe position. Have him keep his balance and throw the bean bags into the can. He can throw either under hand or over hand. Have him do it first with his right hand then his left hand and finally both hands at the same time. Keep score of how many baskets he makes.

Level 3

1. Have the child stand about ten feet in front of the trash can. Have him close his eyes and see if he can throw the bean bag into the can. Keep his score.

Pattern Hopping

Purpose: Motor

Materials: None

Method: The child will do the following activities.

Level 1

1. The child stands in front of you, arms at his side. Have him hop up and down. Make sure both his feet leave and touch the floor at the same time.

2. Have him hop across the room on one foot. Have him do it first with his right foot and then hop back on his left foot.

Level 2

1. Clap a pattern and have him hop to the pattern. For example, one clap, pause and two quick claps would be one hop, pause and two quick hops. Have him do this first, on both feet, then on one foot.

2. Do #1 but have the child facing away from you so he cannot see you clapping.

Level 3

1. Have the child facing you. Clap a pattern. He is to alternate feet as he hops to the pattern. For example, clap, clap, pause, clap, clap clap would be right, left, pause, right, left, right.

Level 4

1. Have the child facing away from you. Clap a pattern. He is to alternate feet and call out which foot he is hopping on as he hops to the pattern. For example, clap, pause, clap, clap, he would hop and call out "right" pause, "left", "right".

Marine Crawl

Purpose: Motor

Materials: None

Method: Child is to be on his stomach with his head looking at a target across the room. At your command he is to crawl forward on his stomach toward the target without taking his eyes off of it. (Figure 1) He is to crawl in such a way that he is pulling with his arm on one side of the body and pushing with his leg on the other side. The target can be anything, for example, a chair or a toy, etc.

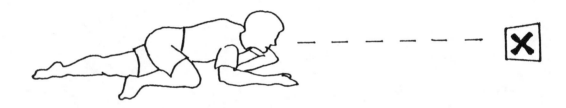

Figure 1

Observations: He is to keep his eyes on the target.

Level 1

1. Have him crawl forward toward the target. Make sure he has good form and is pulling with his arm on one side and pushing with his leg on the other side.

Level 2

1. Same as level 1 but have him also crawl backwards away from the target. For this he will have to push with his arm and bring his opposite leg up to his side.

V.M.C. Bat While Balancing

Purpose: Motor

Materials: V.M.C. Bat, Marsden Ball, Balance Disc

Methods: He does these activities while he is standing on the balance disc or the end of the walking rail.

Level 2

1. Have the child hit the ball by pushing the bat at it. See how long he can do it without missing the ball.

2. You call out various colors on the bat and have him hit the ball with that color.

Level 3

1. Call out a side and color and have the child hit the ball with that color. For example, "right red" or "left blue".

2. Have him hit various colors in sequence. For example, "right red," "left blue", and "right green".

3. Have him hit it a number of times with one color and another number of times with another color. For example, ten times with the "right red" and three times with the "left blue".

Gross Motor Balance Sequence

Purpose: Motor

Materials: None

Method: Child is to do the following activities:

Level 1

1. Have the child assume a hand and knee position on the floor. Have him raise one hand in the air. The goal is to maintain his balance for a count of ten. Do the same but have him raise the other hand in the air.

2. Repeat step one but have the child raise a leg instead of a hand.

3. Repeat step one raising hand and leg on the same side of body.

4. Repeat step one raising hand and leg on opposite sides of body.

Level 2

1. Have the child balance on his tiptoes for a count of ten.

2. Have him rise smoothly and evenly from a sitting position on the floor while keeping his arms folded on his chest.

3. Have him maintain his balance while walking forward and backward on his knees.

4. Have him maintain his balance for a count of ten while standing on one foot. (For children 6 and under maintain balance for a count of five.)

Level 3-A

1. Have him maintain his balance while hopping on one foot with his eyes closed. Repeat with other foot.

2. Have him maintain his balance while jumping with both feet with his eyes closed. He is to make 1/4 or 1/2 turns while jumping.

3. Repeat number 2, but he is to use only one foot. Repeat with other foot.

Level 3-B

1. Have the child stand and maintain his balance while moving his arm and leg on the same side of his body. His arm and leg are to be kept straight and pivoted from the shoulder and hip in an arc to the side.

2. Repeat number 1 but have him use his arm and leg on the opposite side of his body.

Trampoline

Purpose: Motor

Materials: Trampoline, metronome, fixation chart (A small trampoline is adequate.)

Method: On the trampoline have the child do the following:

Level 1

1. Have the child jump on the trampoline, trying to stay in one place. You are looking for good form here with both of his feet touching the trampoline at the same time.

Level 2

1. While the child is jumping, have him catch a beanbag and throw it back to you.

2. While the child is jumping, have him hold a weight in one hand. (A weight can be any small object. For example, a flashlight etc.)

3. Same as #2 but have him swing the weighted hands through various motions as he jumps on the trampoline.

4. As the child jumps, he is to alternate back and forth once on each foot.

5. Have him jump on left foot twice, right foot once. Vary this activity. For example, right foot twice, left foot three times.

Level 3

1. Have the child jump and clap his hands to various rhythmic combinations.

2. Have him jump and call out the letters in a left to right sequence on the fixation chart. Add the metronome and have him call out a letter to each beat of the metronome.

3 Have the child hop and do jumping jacks. He is to keep his arms and legs working together in a synchronized manner.

4. Have him hold a beanbag in each hand and do jumping jacks.

5. Have him do jumping jacks and switch the beanbag from hand to hand when his hands are in the overhead position.

6. As the child is doing jumping jacks, on command have him drop both of his arms without disturbing the total pattern.

7. As the child is doing jumping jacks, on command have him drop just his left or right arm.

Level 4

1. As the child is doing jumping jacks, on command he is to drop his right arm for two jumps, and bring it back for two jumps. Then he is to drop his left arm for two jumps and bring it back for two jumps.

2. Have him jump in a cross pattern. He is to move his right arm and his left leg forward as he moves his left arm and right leg back.

Fixation Chart

1	9	2	1	3	5	4	7
3	8	3	7	6	3	2	5
4	6	5	1	8	6	1	3
5	3	7	3	2	9	4	6
6	4	8	4	1	7	8	2
7	2	9	5	9	3	9	4
8	9	2	7	5	1	6	3
9	5	1	6	3	2	7	4
8	3	5	8	2	1	3	7
5	1	6	7	8	2	4	3

Creeping Activities

Purpose: Motor

Materials: Metronome

Method: All these procedures are done on hands and knees.
For example,

The procedures can be done with either head leading (going forward) or with feet leading (going backward). Each procedure is done in various sequence patterns of hands and knees leaving and touching the ground. Use the following codes for the patterns: LG = leaves ground, TG = touches ground, H= hand, K= knee.

Use the following patterns:

A.   Moving the hands and knees on the same side of the body. For example, right hand then right knee.

   1st Movement   2nd Movement   3rd Movement   4th Movement

   1. HLG   2. KLG   3. HTG   4. KTG

2. KLG   HLG   KTG   HTG
3. H&K together   LG   H&K together   TG

B.   Moving the hands and knees on the opossite sides of the body. For example, left knee then right hand.

        1. HLG   KLG   HTG   KTG
        2. KLG   HLG   KTG   HTG
        3. H&K together LG   H&K together   TG

Level 1

1. At a slow pace have the child practice the pattern in sequences of A & B above. Only go forward.

Level 2

1. At a slow pace have the child practice the pattern sequences A & B above, going forward and backward.

Level 3

1. Using a metronome, have the child do the pattern sequences A & B above going forward and backward to the beat of the metronome. He makes one move for each beat of the metronome.

Level 4

1. Using a metronome, have the child do the pattern sequence A & B above going forward and backward to the beat of the metronome. He is to call out which hand or knee he is lifting off the floor. For example, "right hand" or "left knee".

Crawling Activities

Purpose: Motor

Materials: None

Method: Do these activities with the child lying on his stomach or on his back. Have him keep his head up and looking straight ahead (if he is on his back have him look straight up at the ceiling).

Level 2

1. Have him slide his body along the floor by using only his arms and dragging his legs or only his shoulders and legs and dragging his arms. For example,

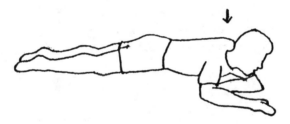

Figure 1

Figure 2

2. Have him use only his hips and shoulder motion and drag his arms and legs. For example,

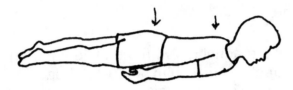

Figure 3

Balance Board-On Hands and Knees

Purpose: Motor

Materials: Marsden ball, balance board, metronome, fixation chart

Method: Have the child get on his hands and knees on the balance board. Make sure he keeps his head up and looks straight ahead.

Level 1

1. Child is to keep his balance on the board as he looks straight ahead. See how long he can keep his balance.

2. Have him move his head back and forth from right to left as he keeps his balance. Hold your thumbs about 24 inches apart and directly in front of him. Have him move his eyes quickly from thumb to thumb.

Level 2

1. Do four corner fixations. Have the child stare straight ahead. At the beat of the metronome he moves his eyes quickly to the top right corner of the wall, then the bottom right corner, then the bottom left corner and then the top left corner. He moves his eyes each time the metronome beats. He is not to move his head, only his eyes.

2. Have him track the Marsden ball in a left to right direction. Have the ball hang so that it is at his eye level. He moves his eyes only, not his head.

3. Swing the ball around his head in a circular fashion and see if he can keep his head and eyes on it without losing his balance.

Level 3

1. Put a number fixation chart directly in front of him on the wall. As he keeps his balance he is to call out the numbers as fast as he can. You can go in the horizontal or vertical direction. He moves his eyes only, not his head.

Fixation Chart

1	9	2	1	3	5	4	7
3	8	3	7	6	3	2	5
4	6	5	1	8	6	1	3
5	3	7	3	2	9	4	6
6	4	8	4	1	7	8	2
7	2	9	5	9	3	9	4
8	9	2	7	5	1	6	3
9	5	1	6	3	2	7	4
8	3	5	8	2	1	3	7
5	1	6	7	8	2	4	3

Letter Tracking and Bouncing a Ball

Purpose: Motor

Materials: Letter chart, playground ball

Method: Have the child slowly walk towards a letter chart hung at his eye level on the wall about 15 feet from him.

Level 1

1. As he walks toward the chart each step he takes he calls out a letter. Have him call out the letters in a left to right sequence. If he doesn't know his letters yet, he takes a step each time you call out and point to a letter.

Level 2

1. As he walks toward the chart, have him call out the leg he is stepping out on first before he calls out the letter. For example, "right leg" then the letter.

2. Have the child bounce a ball as he takes a step and calls out a letter. Have him call out the letters in a left to right sequence. Start by having him just use his right hand and then his left. Have him bounce the ball once for each letter.

3. Alternate between the right and left hands and have him call out which hand he is bouncing the ball with before he calls out the letter.

Level 3

1. Have the child bounce a ball as he takes a step and calls out a letter. Have him call out the letters in a left to right sequence. Vary the number of times he bounces the ball with each hand before he calls out the hand and the letter. For example, one bounce with the right hand as he steps out with his right leg. He then calls out "right" and names the letter. Next have him bounce the ball two times with his left hand as he steps out with his left leg. He then calls out "left" and names a letter. He continues with this sequence until you tell him to stop.

53

Letter Chart

F O D C T P V N

B Y E L Z K O A

T E M K B W F H

X B O M S R T F

A R X E P V S D

P M N B C E A O

R C K P E D B G

X F A D R S M P

M T S G O A X U

O H T U K N C S

55

Walking Rail/Balance Beam

Purpose: Motor

Materials: Walking rail, various objects to carry, book, yardstick, playground ball, and bean bag. You will need an eight-foot long 2"x4" board that has been sanded so there are no rough places. You will need three one foot long 4"x4" blocks of wood. Lay the 2"x4" on the blocks of wood to make the walking rail.

Method: Tell the child to do the following activities.   Also make sure he has good posture with his head up and eyes looking straight ahead. When he walks on the rail have him walk in a heel to toe manner. (Figure 1) His heel should touch his toe on each step. Always have the child take his shoes off and walk on the rail in his socks or bare feet.

If level 2 of this activity is too difficult for the child and he has an extremely difficult time balancing on the board, switch to "Masking Tape Activities".

Figure 1

Level 2-A Tell the child to do the following:

1. Walk forward across the board. (Child keeps his eyes on a target in front of him.)

2. Walk forward across the board and carry a weight in the left hand.

3. Walk forward across the board and carry the weight in the right hand.

4. Walk forward across the board and change the weight from hand to hand.

5. Walk backward across the board.

6. Walk backward across the board and carry a weight in the left hand.

7. Invent your own way to cross the board.

Level 2-B Tell the child to do the following:

1. Walk backward across the board and change the weight from hand to hand.

2. Walk forward across the board with a book balanced on your head.

3. Walk backward across the board and balance a book on your head.

4. Walk forward across the board with a book balanced on your head and carry a weight.

5. Walk across the board and throw a beanbag at a target on command.

Level 2-C Tell the child to do the following:

1. Walk forward across the board and catch a beanbag and throw it back.

2. Walk forward across the board and bounce a ball as you walk.

3. Walk sideways across the board and lead with the right foot.

4. Walk sideways across the board and lead with the left foot.

5. Walk sideways across the board and carry a weight in one of your hands

Level 2-D Tell the child to do the following:

1. Walk sideways across the board and change a weight from hand to hand.

2. Walk sideways across the board with a book balanced on top of your head and carry a weight in your hand.

3. Walk sideways across the board with a weight in your hand. In the middle of the board turn around and walk backward to the end.

4. Walk across the board with your arms extended to the sides; then to the front, back, both to one side, then both to the other side.

5. Walk across the board with your arms extended in front; back to opposite sides and then both to one side, then both to the other side.

Level 2-E Tell the child to do the following:

1. Walk forward with left foot always in front of the right.

2. Walk forward with right foot always in front of the left.

3. Walk backward with right foot always in front of the left.

4. Walk backward with left foot always in front of the right.

5. Invent five activities.

Level 3-A Tell the child to do the following:

1. Walk forward and pick up a book from the center of the beam.

2. Walk backward and pick up a book from the center of the beam.

3. Walk sideways, leading with left side, and pick up a book from the center of the beam.

4. Walk sideways, leading with right side, and pick up a book from the center of the beam.

5. Repeat activities 1-4, but this time pick up the book and place it on top of your head and continue to the end of the board.

Level 3-B Tell the child to do the following:

1. Have someone hold a yardstick 12 inches over the center of the beam. Walk to the center and step over the yardstick.

2. Increase the height of the step necessary to clear the yardstick.

3. Walk across the beam in various ways. Have someone stand at the end of the board with a target. Watch the target as you move across the beam.

4. Repeat #3 but keep your eyes on the target as the target is moved. (Call it to his attention if he loses the target or if his eyes look away.)

Level 3-C Tell the child to do the following:

1. Invent seven ways to cross the board that have not been covered.

2. Teacher or parent holds a yardstick at a height of three feet. Walk forward and pass under the yardstick.

3. Child is to now go under and over the yardstick. (Teacher varies the position of the yardstick both in height and in position relative to the length of the beam.)

Level 3-D Tell the child to do the following:

1. Walk the beam forward with your arms out, palms down with a book on the back of each hand.

2. Same as #1 but walk the beam backwards.

3. Invent five ways to cross the board using the books balanced on your hands.

Level 3-E Tell the child to do the following:

1. Walk the board in various directions with all of your weight being carried on the balls of your feet.

2. Walking on the balls of your feet, carry various weights across the board and change the position of the weights as you walk.

3. Invent three new ways to cross the board.

Level 3-F Tell the child to do the following:

1. Go to the center of board. Catch a beanbag and throw it back to the teacher or parent or at a target. Move to various positions on the board and repeat throwing the beanbag. (Teacher or parent remains in one place.)

2. Go to the center of the board. (Teacher or parent goes to the end of the beam where the child will be facing her.) Move arms and legs in various positions exactly as teacher or parent does. (If child's position is not correct, call his attention to the fact.)

3. (Teacher or parent places a bucket at the end of the beam and throws the child a beanbag.) Walk towards the bucket, catch the beanbag and try to throw the beanbag into the bucket without looking at it.

Level 3-G Tell the child to do the following:

1. Place a book at the middle of the beam. Walk the beam sideways and pick up the book, turn around and walk to the end of the beam.

2. Invent seven ways to cross the beam using all three of the items. (the yardstick, the book and the beanbag)

3. (Teacher or parent holds the yardstick at various heights above the beam.) Put your hands on your hips and walk backward and go under the yardstick.

Level 3-H Tell the child to do the following:

1. With your arms held sideways, walk to the middle of the beam, turn around and walk backward.

2. Walk forward to the middle of the beam, then turn and walk the remaining distance sideways left with your weight on the balls of your feet.

3. Walk to the center of beam, then turn and continue sideways right.

4. Walk forward with hands on hips.

5. Walk backward with hands on hips.

6. Place book at center of beam. Walk to center, place the book on the top of your head, and then continue to end of beam.

Level 3-I Tell the child to do the following:

1. Walk backward and pass under yardstick held by the teacher or parent.

2. Walk the beam backward with your hands clasped behind your body.

3. Walk the beam forward, arms held sideways, palms up, with a book on the palm of each hand.

4. Walk the beam backward, arms held sideways, palms up, with a book on the palm of each hand.

5. Walk the beam sideways, right, weight on balls of feet.

6. Walk the beam sideways, left, weight on balls of feet.

Level 4-A Tell the child to do the following:

1. Hop on the right foot the full length of the beam.

2. Hop on the left foot the full length of the beam.

3. Hop halfway on the right foot and halfway on the left foot.

4. Hop back and forth on the beam, alternating the left and the right foot.

5. Skip the full length of the beam.

6. Clasp arms in rear and walk across the board.

Level 4-B Tell the child to do the following:

1. Invent seven different ways to cross the board with arms in various positions.

2. Invent seven different ways to cross the board with one arm held in various positions.

3. Walk to the center of the board, stand on the left foot and balance.

4. Repeat #3, but balance on the right foot.

Level 4-C Tell the child to do the following:

1. Hop to the center of the beam and turn around, hop backward to the end.

2. Invent two activities using the hop and the yardstick.

3. Walk to the center of the board. Close your eyes and walk to the end.

4. Walk to the center of the beam. Then close your eyes and see how long your balance can be maintained. (Record the number of seconds child's balance is maintained.)

5. Walk to the center of the board, close your eyes, stand on your toes and see how long your balance can be maintained. (Record the number of seconds his balance is maintained.)

6. Devise five activities with the eyes closed.

Level 4-D Tell the child to do the following:

1. Walk to the middle of the beam. Balance on one foot then turn around on that foot and walk backwards to the end of the beam.

2. Walk to the middle of the beam, left sideways, turn around and walk to end of the beam, right sideways.

3. With yours arms clasped behind your body, walk forward to the middle, turn around once, walk backward the remaining distance.

Level 4-E Tell the child to do the following:

1. (Teacher or parent holds yardstick six inches above beam, balance a book on the child's head.) Walk forward stepping over the yardstick.

2. (Teacher or parent holds yardstick 15 inches above the beam, balance a book on the child's head.) Walk forward stepping over the yardstick.

3. (Teacher or parent holds yardstick 15 inches above the beam, balance a book on the child's head.) Walk sideways right, stepping over the yardstick.

4. (Teacher or parent holds yardstick 15 inches above the beam, balance a book on the child's head.) Walk sideways left, stepping over the yardstick.

5. (Teacher or parent holds yardstick three feet high.) Walk forward with your hands on your hips and pass under the stick.

Level 5 Tell the child to do the following:

1. Stand on beam, one foot in front of the other, keep your eyes closed and maintain your balance as long as possible. (Record number of seconds.)

2. Stand on your right foot, eyes closed, and maintain your balance as long as possible. (Record number of seconds.)

3. Stand on your left foot, eyes closed and maintain your balance as long as possible. (Record number of seconds.)

4. Walk beam sideways, left eye closed.

Tape Walking

Purpose: Motor

Materials: Masking tape

Method: Put an eight foot long strip of fairly wide masking tape on the floor. The child is to do the following activities walking in a heel to toe manner on the tape. He is to walk so that the heel of one foot touches the toes of the other. He is not to have his shoes on and should always have good posture and keep his head and eyes straight ahead.

Level 1-A Tell the child to do the following:

1. Walk forward on the tape. (Child keeps his eyes on a target in front of him.)

2. Walk forward on the tape and carry a weight in your left hand.

3. Walk forward on the tape and carry the weight in your right hand.

4. Walk forward on the tape and change the weight from hand to hand.

5. Walk backward on the tape.

6. Walk backward on the tape and carry a weight in your left hand.

7. Invent your own way to cross the tape.

Level 1-B Tell the child to do the following:

1. Walk backward on the tape and change the weight from hand to hand.

2. Walk forward on the tape with a book balanced on your head.

3. Walk backward on the tape and balance a book on your head.

4. Walk on the tape with a book balanced on your head and carry a weight.

5. Walk on the tape and throw a beanbag at a target on command.

Level 1-C Tell the child to do the following:

1. Walk on the tape and catch a beanbag and throw it back.

2. Walk on the tape and bounce a ball as you walk.

3. Walk sideways on the tape and lead with your right foot.

4. Walk sideways on the tape and lead with your left foot.

5. Walk sideways on the tape and carry a weight in one of your hands.

Level 1-D Tell the child to do the following:

1. Walk sideways on the tape and change a weight from hand to hand.

2. Walk sideways on the tape with a book balanced on top of your head and carry a weight in your hand.

3. Walk sideways on the tape with a weight in your hand. In the middle of the tape turn around and walk backward to the end.

4. Walk on the tape with your arms extended to the sides; then to the front, back, both to one side, and then both to the other side.

5. Walk on the tape with your arms extended in front; back to opposite sides and then both to one side, and then both to the other side.

Level 1-E Tell the child to do the following:

1. Walk forward with your left foot always in front of the right.

2. Walk forward with your right foot always in front of the left.

3. Walk backward with your right foot always in front of the left.

4. Walk backward with your left foot always in front of the right.

5. Invent five activities.

Beanbag Activities

Purpose: Motor

Materials: Beanbags

Method: Tell the child to do the following activities:

Level 2-A

1. Throw the beanbag up in the air with both hands and catch it when it comes back down. Make the two sides of your body move exactly the same way.

2. Throw and catch the beanbag with both hands. Make the beanbag just touch the ceiling.

3. Throw and catch the beanbag with both hands. Try to make it come as close to the ceiling as you can without touching the ceiling.

Level 2-B

1. Throw and catch the beanbag with both hands. Throw the beanbag up and try to make it come one foot from the ceiling, then two feet from the ceiling, and then three feet from the ceiling. Continue this sequence.

2. Throw and catch the beanbag with the right hand and follow the motion of the beanbag with your eyes. Keep your eyes on the beanbag throughout its trajectory.

3. Throw and catch the beanbag with your left hand. Follow the motion of the beanbag with your eyes. Keep your eyes on the beanbag throughout its trajectory.

Level 3-A

1. Throw and catch the beanbag with your right hand. Make the beanbag just touch the ceiling as you throw it.

2. Throw and catch the beanbag with your left hand. Make the beanbag just touch the ceiling when you throw it.

3. Throw and catch the beanbag with your right hand. Make the beanbag come as close to the ceiling as you can without touching the ceiling.

4. Throw and catch the beanbag with your left hand. Make the beanbag come as close to the ceiling as you possibly can without touching the ceiling.

Level 3-B

1. Throw and catch the beanbag with your right hand. Make the beanbag come to within one foot of the ceiling. The next time make it come within two feet of the ceiling. The next time make it come within three feet of the ceiling.

2. Throw and catch the beanbag with your left hand. Make the beanbag come to within one foot of the ceiling. The next time make it come within two feet of the ceiling. The next time make it come within three feet of the ceiling. Continue this sequence.

Level 4-A

1. Throw and catch the beanbag with both hands. Make the beanbag come as close to the ceiling as possible when you throw it up and let it get as close to the floor as possible before you catch it.

2. Throw the beanbag with your left hand. Make the beanbag come as close to the ceiling as possible when you throw it up and let it get as close to the floor as possible before you catch it. Catch it with your left hand.

3. Throw the beanbag up with your right hand. Make the beanbag come as close to the ceiling as possible when you throw it up and let it get as close to the floor as possible before you catch it. Catch it with your right hand.

4. Invent your own way to throw and catch the beanbag.

Level 4-B

1. Throw the beanbag up in the air with your right hand. Catch it with both hands when it comes back down. The first time you throw it up, let it get as close to the ceiing as you can. The second time throw it to within one foot of the ceiling and the third time throw it within two feet of the ceiling.

2. Throw the beanbag up in the air with your left hand. Catch it with both hands when it comes back down. The first time you throw it up, let it get as close to the ceiling as you can. The second time throw it to within one foot of the ceiling and the third time throw it within two feet of the ceiling.

3. Throw the beanbag up in the air with your right hand. Catch it with your right hand when it comes back down. Catch it as high in the air as you can.

4. Throw the beanbag up in the air with your left hand. Catch it with your right hand when it comes back down. Catch it as high up in the air as you can.

Level 4-C

1. Throw the beanbag up in the air with your right hand. Let it get as close to the floor as you can before you catch it with your left hand.

2. Throw it with your left hand and catch it with your right hand. Let it get as close to the floor as possible before you catch it.

3. Throw it with your left hand and catch it with your right hand. Catch it at eye level.

Level 5

1. Throw the beanbag up with both hands and catch it on the back of your right hand when it comes back down.

2. Throw the beanbag up with both hands and catch it on the back of your left hand when it comes back down.

3. Put the beanbag on the back of both hands. Throw the beanbag up in the air and catch it.

4. Throw the bag in the air and when it reaches its trajectory close your eyes. Try to catch the beanbag with your eyes closed.

5. Throw and catch two beanbags simultaneously. Throw and catch the lightest beanbag with your right hand and the heaviest beanbag with your left hand.

6. Throw and catch two beanbags simultaneously. Throw and catch the heaviest beanbag with your right hand and the lightest beanbag with your left hand.

7. Throw and catch two beanbags simultaneously. Throw the heaviest one with your left hand and the lightest one with your right hand. Throw them as high up in the air as you can and keep them under control. Try to throw them up and just touch the ceiling. Try to make both of them go up the same distance when you throw them.

8. Throw the two bags in the air and clap a rhythm pattern before catching the bags.

9. Throw the two bags. Clap your hands and slap your legs before you catch the bags.

Colored Squares[62]

Purpose: Motor

Materials: Carpet squares, tile squares or plastic squares, metronome

Method: Arrange a large pattern of colored squares on the floor. For example,

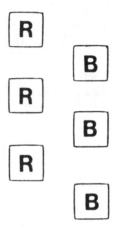

Color code the child's feet, one color for each foot. For example, his right foot is coded red and his left foot blue.

Level 1

1. Color code the child's feet separate colors. Have him walk through the colored squares only on those that match his color coded feet. For example, tell him that his right foot is red and his left foot is green. Vary the codes for his feet.

Level 2

1. Have the child hop one foot at a time and land on the squares that are the same color as the colors coded for his feet. For example, code his left foot blue. He is to hop only on the blue squares with his left foot.

2. Code each foot and have him hop alternating between feet to the correct color.

3. Add a metronome. Each time he hears the metronome beat, he will alternate feet and hop to a different square. Make sure he only hops on the square that is the same color as the color you assigned to his foot.

Level 3

1. Tell the child the sequence you want him to hop. For example, hop three times on the right foot and two on the left. Each time he hears the metronome beat he will hop to the colored square that is the same color as the color that his foot is coded.

2. Vary the color code for the feet and the sequences. For example,

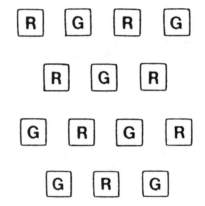

Clothespins

Purpose: Motor

Materials: Clothespins (the kind that you pinch together to open)

Method: Have the child do the following activities.

Level 1

1. Have the child pinch the clothespin with different fingers and thumb.

2. Repeat the pinching action five times with each finger on each hand. The arm may be held in different positions as pinching occurs. For example, over the head, to the left, behind the back, behind the knees, etc.

3. When he is good at manipulating the clothespin, try to have him pick up objects such as marbles, sticks, etc.

Level 2

1. Same as Level 1, but have the child hold a clothespin in each hand and do both hands at the same time.

Activities For Ball Bouncing[63]

Purpose: Motor

Materials: Playground ball (ball about 4" to 5" in diameter that has a good bounce), colored tape, metronome

Method: Have the child do the following activities.

Level 1

1. Have the child use one or both hands, whatever is comfortable. Put the child in a sitting position. Have him bounce the ball between his legs. Begin with small gentle bounces and increase vigor.

Level 2

1. Alternating hands while standing still.

   a. Begin with ball in right hand. Bounce it close to the feet and in front. As the ball rebounds, force it down again with left hand. Bounce the ball alternating hands as long as possible.

   b. Begin different rhythmic patterns of ball bouncing. For example, start with ball in left hand. As it rebounds from the floor use this pattern: 2R, 1 Both, 2L, 1 Both, 2R. Some other patterns could be: 2 Both, 1L, 3R, 3L or 1R, 2 Both, 2L, 1R, 2 Both.

   c. Complete both a and b series while walking.

   d. Use different degrees of force while standing still or moving.

   e. Create different walking patterns.

Level 3

1. Have the child alternate hands as he does these activities.

   a. Make three 48" circles from colored tape on the floor. For example, red, green, and blue. Child must bounce the ball within the restricted circle. Each circle is coded. For example, blue indicates bouncing with both hands; red indicates right hand; and green indicates left hand. Child moves from each circle changing activity according to the code.

   b. Make three 30" squares from colored tape on the floor. For example. white, black, and yellow .The child must bounce the ball within the square according to each color's particular code. White indicates an alternating hand bounce: R,L,R,L ....; black indicates the pattern: 1 both hands, 2L, 2R, 1 both hands; yellow indicates the pattern: 1L, 2R, 1 both hands.

   c. On the floor are 30" X 15" rectangles that are divided in half to make two 15" squares. Child stands in one 15" square and bounces the ball within the limits of the other 15" square. Use various patterns starting with simple to complex. For example,

      1. as many as possible with both hands.
      2. as many as possible with left hand.
      3. as many as possible with right hand.
      4. alternating L, R, L, R, L.
      5. both hands, 2L, 2R, 1L, 2 both.

Level 4

1. Same as level three but a metronome is added. Set the pattern to a constant rhythm by use of a metronome. Child bounces the ball each time the metronome beats.

2. Create a course with different squares, circles, lines. Include places where child doesn't bounce the ball, but hops. For example, in all triangle shapes he holds the ball and hops on one foot, square shapes he holds the ball and hops on both feet.

Jump Rope Activities

Purpose: Motor

Materials: 7' jump rope, metronome

Method: The child should do all these activities with relaxed knees, a straight but not stiff back and his head held up. If the child cannot swing the rope himself and jump at the same time, tie one end to a chair and you swing the other end for him.

Level 1 Do these activities with the rope laying on the floor.

1. With the rope laying in a straight line, have the child place a foot on either side of the rope and jump to the opposite end forward and return to the starting end with a backward jump.

2. With the rope in a circle, jump with feet together in and out of the circle.

3. With the rope in a circle, place one hand on the floor inside the circle and walk around the outside until you return to the starting point.

4. With the rope in a circle, place one foot on the inside and the other on the outside of the circle. Jump around the circle to the starting place.

Level 2 One end of the rope is in each hand.

1. Swing the rope back and forth under the body and jump with feet together each time it goes under the body.

2. Same as #1 but use only the right foot.

3. Same as #1 but use only the left foot.

4. Swing the rope over the head and under the body, jumping each time it goes under the body. Jump with both feet at the same time.

Level 3 One end of the rope is in each hand.

1. Swing the rope over the head and under the body, jumping each time it goes under the body. Jump with both feet at the same time. Do one jump for each beat of the metronome. Set the metronome at a very slow cadence for this activity and then work up the speed.

2. Same as #1 but alternate feet for each beat.

SECTION II

VISUAL MOTOR THERAPY PROCEDURES

Pencil Grip Relaxation

Purpose: Visual motor

Materials: Pencil and paper

Method: These activities are designed for the child who has a tight pencil grip or seems very tense during reading or writing.

Level 2

1. Have the child sit in a chair and at your command make a fist as tightly as he can. Have him hold it for the count of 10. Then have him relax his fist for the count of 10. Have him do this five times. Make him aware that he needs to relax while he is drawing or writing.

2. After he does number 1, see how lightly the child can draw a line on a piece of paper. The object is to have him draw a line that is just barely visible.

Flashlight Activities

Purpose: Visual Motor

Materials: Two flashlights

Method: Turn the lights in the room down. You don't want it completely dark.

Level 1

1. Name an object in the room. See how quickly the child can push the "on" button, aim the flashlight and shine it on the object you called out.

2. Have the child move the light in circles and other figure patterns on the wall. Do first with his right hand then with his left.

Level 2

1. Both you and the child have a flashlight. Shine your light on the wall in different geometric shapes or number or letter patterns. The child must keep his light on yours. When you have finished, ask him what pattern, number or letter you drew with your light.

Mirror Image Activities

Purpose: Visual Motor

Materials: 7 x 10 inch mirror, pencils, and paper

Method: Two pencils are held together to draw a double line which looks like a race track. (Figure 1) Start with one or two curves with the lines not too close together. Later you can add curves and narrow the track. The child sits looking into the mirror placed in front of him at a right angle to the paper and parallel to his body. (Figure 2) The paper with the track drawn on it is on the table. Try not to have the writing hand touch the paper, only the tip of the pencil.

Figure 1

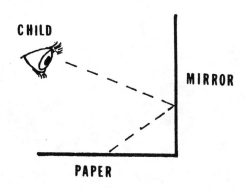

Figure 2

Level 3

1. The child is to look into the mirror and draw a line that stays within the track lines. If he goes out of the lines, he is to find his way back without lifting the pencil from the paper.

2. Turn the paper 90 degrees and have him go top to bottom.

Level 4

1. Put a series of dots randomly on the paper. The child is to connect all the dots. He must not lift his pencil from the paper.

Dot Pattern Designs

Purpose: Visual Motor

Materials: Blackboard

Method: Draw rows of dots on the blackboard to form a dot pattern. Draw a geometric shape by connecting some of the dots. The child is to duplicate your geometric shape by connecting the same dots with his own dot pattern.   As you proceed from Level 2 to Level 5 you will gradually start to eliminate dots so that the child has less reinforcement to help him.   When possible, have the child draw the shapes from top to bottom, and left to right. Have him describe the direction he is drawing each line. For example, top to bottom or left to right. Start with five rows of five dots. For example,

The child should be able to do the following geometric shapes in each level before going to the next level.

Level 2

1. Make the basic shapes and letters as shown above. Use five rows of five dots. For example,

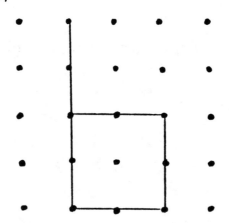

2. Make up your own shapes.
3. When the child can copy them correctly on the blackboard, have him do it on a piece of paper.

Level 3-A

1. Make the basic shapes and letters as shown. Use the following dot pattern. For example,

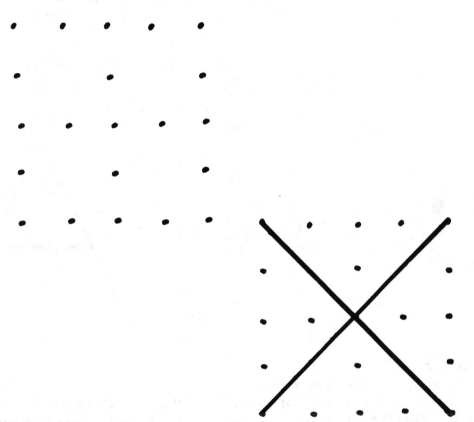

2. Make up your own shapes.

3. When the child can copy them correctly on the board, have him do it on a piece of paper.

Level 3-B

1. Make the basic shapes and letters as shown. Use the following dot pattern. For example,

2. Make up your own shapes.

3. When the child can copy them correctly on the board, have him do it on a piece of paper.

Level 4

1. Make the basic shapes and letters as shown. Use the following dot pattern. For example,

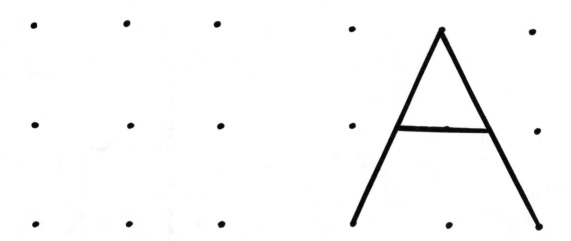

2. Make up your own shapes.

3. Have the child do the shapes on paper instead of the board.

Level 5

1. Make the basic shapes and letters as shown. Use the following dot pattern. For example,

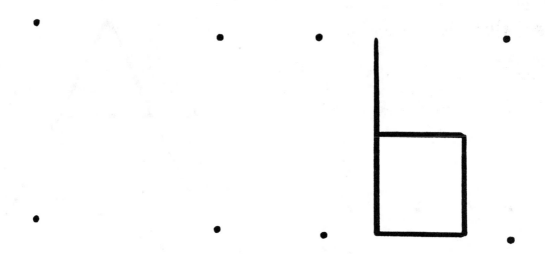

2. Make up your own shapes.

3. Have the child do the shapes on paper instead of the board.

Finish the Designs

Purpose: Visual Motor

Materials: Blackboard

Method: The child is to finish on the blackboard the designs in B to look like A. Do the following designs and then make up your own. For example,

A   B

S   S

8   8

∞   ∞

b   b

Z   Z

d   d

A   A

Level 1

1. Do the designs above. Vary the missing parts. When the child has completed these, make up your own. Use as many letters as possible.

2. Draw the designs on a sheet of paper instead of the board.

93

Level 2

1. Use the designs on the previous page in combinations. Vary the missing parts. For example,

A   B

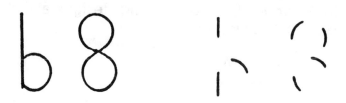

When you have used as many combinations as possible, make up your own. Use as many letters as possible.

2. Draw the designs on a sheet of paper instead of the board.

Can You Imagine a Shape?

Purpose: Visual motor

Materials: Blackboard

Method: Put some numbers on the board to form a pattern. Give the child a numbered sequence. He is to follow the sequence with only his eyes and tell you which geometric shape it would be if he drew a line in the sequence you gave him. If he has trouble doing it with just his eyes, let him use his finger and trace the sequence. If he still has trouble, let him trace it with chalk. Vary the number patters. For example,

```
1        2                    1
                  or    4        2
4        3                    3
```

Example 1A,

```
1        2

4        3
```

Sequence 1 2 3 4 1 would be which shape?

a   **b**   **c**

Answer is A since the sequence is

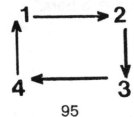

Example 1B,

Sequence 1, 3, 4 would be which of these shapes?

a   b   c

Answer is C since sequence is

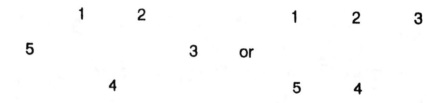

Level 2

1. Have the child trace the sequence in chalk and then point to the correct shape. Use a maximum of four numbers.

Level 3

1. Have the child trace the sequence in the air with his finger and tell you the correct shape. If he has difficulty, let him trace it with chalk on the blackboard. Use a maximum of 5 numbers. Vary the number patterns.

For example,

       1   2   1   2   3

5   3   or

     4   5   4

Level 4

1. Have the child trace the pattern with his eyes only and identify the correct shape. If he has difficulty, let him trace it in the air with his finger. Use a maximum of 5 numbers.

For example,

1   2

        5

    4   3   sequence 1 2 3 4 5 1

            would be,

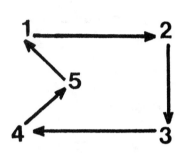

Level 5

1. Have the child trace the pattern with his eyes only and identify the correct shape. Use a maximum of 6 numbers. Vary the number pattern.

Geoboards

Purpose: Visual Motor

Materials: 2 geoboards, rubber bands, blackboard. A geoboard is a square piece of wood 4"x 4" and 1" thick. Hammer nails in the wood so that they are evenly spaced and in rows.   For example,

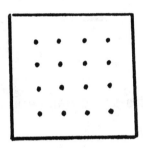

Method: To make patterns with the geoboards stretch rubber bands over the nails. For example,

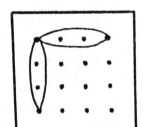

Level 1

1. Have the child copy on his geoboard the pattern you make with your geoboard. Do not use more than two rubberbands. For example,

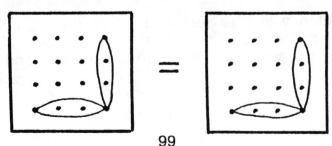

99

Level 2

1. Have the child copy on his geobard the pattern you make with your geoboard. Use up to four rubber bands. For example,

The child must use the same nails you use to make his pattern.

Level 3

1. Have the child copy on the blackboard the pattern you make with your geoboard. Use up to five rubber bands. For example,

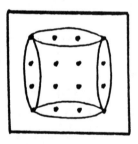

Put dots on the blackboard in the same pattern that you have on your geoboard. He must connect the same dots on the board as the nails your rubber bands cover.

Level 4

1. Make a pattern with your geoboard. Show the child your board for a few seconds and then hide it from him. He must remember the pattern and make it on his geoboard. Use up to four rubber bands.

Level 5

1. Make a pattern with your geoboard. The child must make the mirror image of your pattern with his geoboard. For example,

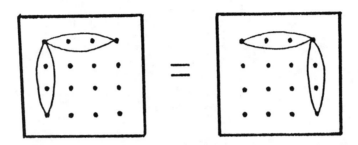

Handwriting Development ⁶⁶

Purpose: Visual Motor

Materials: Chalkboard, pencil and paper, Proper Stroke Sequence Chart

Method: The child is to stand in front of the chalkboard and do the designs that are listed below. Allow the child to do each design as large or small as he wants. Observe body posture, grasp of chalk, rhythmical movement of arm and head, and size of the drawings. Provide help where the child is having trouble. Once the child can do these movements on the blackboard have him practice them on unlined paper.
For example,

1.

2.

3.

4.

5.

6.

7.

8.

9.

10.

11.

12.

13.

14.

15.

16.

17. little to big   a. 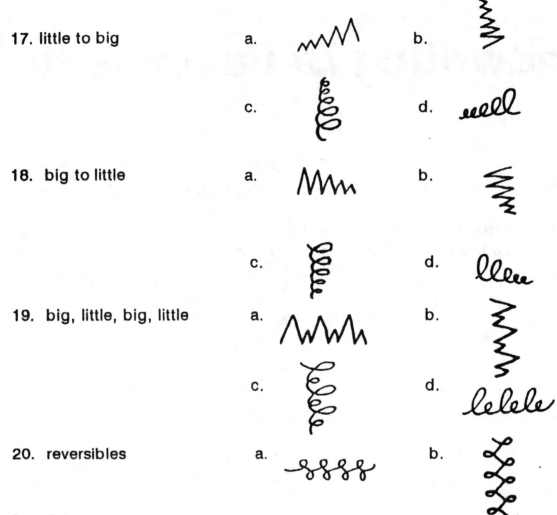   b.

           c.   d.

18. big to little   a.   b.

           c.   d.

19. big, little, big, little   a.   b.

           c.   d.

20. reversibles   a.   b.

Level 2

1. Child will do all the activities on the blackboard.

2. Practice first with one hand and then the other.

Level 3

1. A child will do all the activities on unlined paper.

2. Once the child can do all of the above activities, have him practice the proper stroke sequences for letters. Have him first draw the letters on the blackboard and then on unlined paper. When he can draw them correctly on unlined paper, have him use lined paper.

Proper Stroke Sequences

A a — B b — C c — D d

E e — F f — G g — H h

I i — J j — K k — L l

M m — N n — O o — P p

Q q — R r — S s — T t

U u — V v — W w — X x

Y y — Z z

Controlled Form

Purpose: Visual Motor

Materials: Chalkboard, pencil and paper

Method: Draw boundary lines. (horizontal or vertical) Have the child draw the designs. Encourage him not to go over the lines, but see if he can draw his lines between and just touching the boundary lines. The following activities will be used:

Level 1

    1. Child only does the vertical, horizontal and diagonal lines.

Level 2

    1. Child does all activities through number 8.

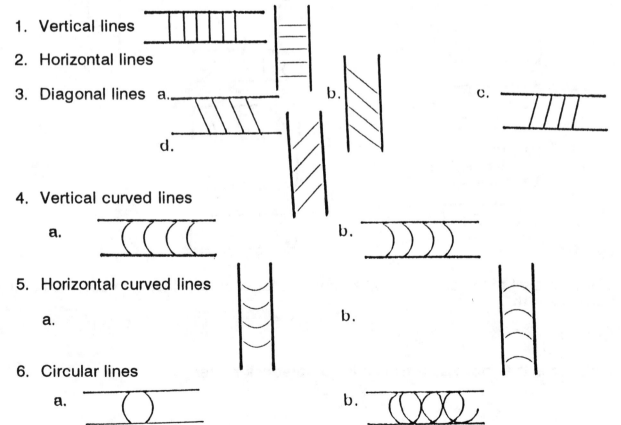

1. Vertical lines

2. Horizontal lines

3. Diagonal lines   a.   b.   c.

     d.

4. Vertical curved lines

    a.   b.

5. Horizontal curved lines

    a.   b.

6. Circular lines

    a.   b.

7. Diagonal lines connected

a.

b.

8. Waves

a.

b.

9. Loops

a.

b.

c.

d.

e.

f.

10. Loops between lines and sections

a.

b.

c.

d.

e.

f.

g.

h.

Level 3.

Child does all of the above activities on the blackboard. Have him use the hand he writes with.

Level 4

Child does the above activities on lined notebook paper.

Eye-Hand and Fine Motor Control

Purpose: Visual Motor

Materials: Pencil, worksheet with X's and O's typed on it
(Figure 1-pg. 111)

Method: With a pencil held in such a fashion that only the point is
touching the paper (no part of the hand to touch),   a
continuous line is drawn over all X's and under all O's in each
line. For example,

X X X X O O O O X X O O X

Level 2

1. Use the preferred hand. Be careful to draw the line in such a way that it
does not touch any of the letters.

2. Use the non-preferred hand.

3. Vary the activity by having the child underline every other group of O's,
etc.

4. When he gets good at this, use a page from a magazine and have him
draw over the first O and then under the second O and back over the
third O, etc. until he gets to the end of the page.

Figure 1.

EYE-HAND WORK SHEET

```
x x x x x o o o x x x o o o o x x o o o o o x x x x x o o
x x o o o x x x x x o o o o o x o o o x x x o o o x x x x
o o o o x x x x x o o x x x x o o o o o x x x x x o o x x x o
x x o o o x x o o o x x x x x o x o o o o o x x x o o o x x
o o o o x x x x x o o x x o x o o o o o x x x o o o x x x x
 x x x x o o o o o o x x x x o o o o x x o o o x x x x o o o
o x x x x x o o o o o x x x x o x o o o o x x x o o o o x x
o o o o o o x x x x x o o o o x x o o x x x o x x x o o o
x x x o o x x x x x x o o o o x x x x o o o x x x x x x o o

o o o o o x x o o o x x x x x o o o o x x o o o o o x x x
x x x x x x o o o o o x x o o o o x x x x x o o o x x x o o
x x x x o o o o o o x x x x o o o o o x x x x x o o x x x x
x x o o o o o x x x x x o o x o o o o o x x x o o o o o o o
x x x o o x x x x x x o o o o x x x o o o x x x x x x o o o
 o o x x x x x o o o o x o o o o x x x x o o o o x x x x x
o o o o x x x x x x x o o x x x o o o o o x x x x o o x x
x x x x o o o o o x x o o o o x x x x x o o o o o x x o o o o
x x o o o x x x x x o o o o o x x o o o x x x x o o x x x
o o o x x x o o o x x x x x o x o o o o o x x x o o o o o o
```

111

Bean Counting

Purpose: Visual Motor

Materials: Pint size jar filled with dried lima beans, tin can, metronome

Method: Have the child do the following activities.

Level 1

1. Have the child count out fifty beans with his right hand and place them in the tin can.

2. Spread the beans on the table and with his left hand have the child put them back in the jar. Repeat using the right hand.

3. Have him pick out fifty beans alternating between the right and the left hand as fast as he can and put them on the table.

Level 2

1. At the beat of a metronome he is to alternate his hands and take the beans out of the can and put them on the table. He then puts them back. You may increase the metronome speed but make sure he only touches the beans each time he hears the metronome beat.

Nuts and Bolts

Purpose: Visual Motor

Materials: Nuts and bolts of various sizes

Method: Have the child do the following activities.

Level 1

1. Have the child remove all the nuts from the bolts. Mix them up and have the child put the nuts back on the bolts as quickly as possible.

Level 2

1. Have the child do the same as level 1, but with his eyes closed.

Line Drawing

Purpose: Visual Motor

Materials: Blackboard

Method: Have the child experience parts of geometric shapes by drawing the following on the blackboard:

1. Lines going uphill
2. Lines going downhill
3. Lines that start at the left edge and go to the right edge
4. Lines near the top and near the bottom
5. Diagonal lines
6. Lines that crisscross
7. Lines that bump each other
8. Curved lines
9. Circles

Level 1

1. The child should use first his right hand and then his left.

2. Show the child how letters can be formed from these various lines.

SECTION III

OCULAR MOTOR THERAPY PROCEDURES

Fixation Activities

Purpose: Ocular Motor

Materials: Blackboard, metronome

Method: For these activities the child is only to move his eyes.   There should not be any head or body movement. Do these activities at first one eye at a time. (Cover his other eye) When he can do the activities without difficulty one eye at a time, have him do both eyes together.

Level 1

1. Have the child sit with his arms extended in front of him and thumbs up. At your command he is to shift his eyes accurately and quickly from one thumb to the other. Have him continue going back and forth between thumbs. Make sure he does not move his head or body.

2. Have the child seated at a table with his hands folded in front of him, thumbs up. The child looks at an object to the left of his thumb, then his left thumb, right thumb and an object to the right of his right thumb. Always go in a left to right direction.

3. Draw two X's on the blackboard at eye level about three feet apart. Have the child stand centered between the two X's and about two feet in front of the board. At the beat of the metronome have him quickly move his eyes back and forth from one X to the other.

Level 2

1. Have the child seated at a table. At the beat of the metronome he is to look quickly from an object on the wall to the left of his table, to an object on the table, to an object on the wall to the right of the table. The table should be about 15 to 20 feet from the wall. Vary the number of objects. Make sure he moves his eyes only, not his head or body.

Four Corner Fixation

Purpose: Ocular Motor

Materials: Chalkboard, metronome

Method: The child will stand approximately five feet from an X drawn on the blackboard at eye level. Set the metronome at about 60 beats a minute. He is to move his eyes only, not his head or body.

Level 1

1. Without the metronome, point to the corners you want him to look at. For example, when you point to the top right corner he will move his eyes quickly and accurately to the top right corner. He then moves his eyes back to the center when you tell him and waits for your next instruction.

Level 2

1. The child will look at the center target for four beats, then on a corner of the chalkboard for four beats, then to the center target for four beats, then the next corner for four beats. This is done until he has looked at all four corners. Start with the top right and work to bottom right, bottom left and top left.

2. Have him repeat #1 but he is to call out the direction of the corners as he looks at them. For example, "top right", "bottom right", etc.

Level 3

1. Set metronome to about 30 beats a minute. At the first beat he calls out the direction he is to move his eyes. For example, top right and look at that corner, points to the corner on the second beat, puts his arm down on the third beat and looks at the center "X" on the fourth beat.

V.M.C. Bat

Purpose: Ocular Motor

Materials: V.M.C. (visual motor control) bat, Marsden Ball

The V.M.C. bat is a dowel rod about three feet long and one inch in diameter. It is divided into various colored sections. For example,

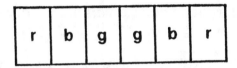

Method: Have the Marsden ball hanging in front of the child, chest high. He is to hold the bat horizontally in front of himself with the top of his hands on top of the bat. For example,

Level 1

1. Have the child hit the ball by pushing the bat at it. See how long he can do it. See how long he can do it without missing the ball.

2. You call out various colors on the bat and have him hit the ball with that color.

Level 2

1. Call out a side and color and have the child hit the ball with that color. For example, "right red" or "left blue".

2. Have him hit various colors in sequence. For example, "right red", "left blue", and "right green".

3. Have him hit it a number of times with one color and another number of times with another color. For example, ten times with the "right red" and three times with the "left blue".

Marsden Ball

Purpose: Ocular Motor

Materials: Marsden ball, letter chart, eye patch

Method: Have the child keep his eye on the ball at all times. Only in the "Dodge Ball" procedure does he not keep his eyes on the ball. In Level 2, he is not to move his head, only his eyes. In all procedures except Level 2, hang the ball from the ceiling so that it is at shoulder height and he is standing about two feet from it.

Level 2

1. The child is to lay down on his back with the ball about two feet directly over his face. Swing the ball in a left to right direction. The child is to keep his eyes on the ball and not move his head or body. Do not swing the ball too fast or too far out. Do this exercise at first with one of the child's eyes covered with an eye patch. Only when he can do each eye individually, have him use both eyes at the same time.

2. Swing the ball left to right, circular, diagonal, head to toe.

Level 3

1. Child is to hit the ball with his hand while he is standing up. Alternate hands and have him call out which hand he is hitting the ball with.

Level 4

1. Dodge Ball: The ball is suspended on a string so the height is just enough to clear the shoulder. The child stands directly under the hook in the ceiling and faces a letter chart. Swing the ball from his front to back on his midline. He must shift his head when the ball swings in front of him to behind him, and when it goes from behind him to his front. For example,

He says a letter on the chart each time it passes his ear. As the ball keeps swinging, it gradually changes its direction and begins to swing from side to side. Do not stop the ball and redirect it. His head should be tilted forward and backward to miss the ball. The child continues to read the letters for as long as he can without being hit by the ball.

2. This procedure is "sequencing the Marsden ball". The ball is suspended at shoulder height so that the shoulder can hit it. The two shoulders, elbows and hands are used to hit the ball. A sequence is given and the child is to say it out loud and then hit the ball with the parts of the body in the proper sequence. For example, "right shoulder", "right hand". Increase the instructions up to six if he can do it.

Level 5

1. Have the child hit the ball with his hand and stomp the foot on the same side as he hits the ball. Have him call out "right" or "left" depending on which side he is using. When he can do this, have him hit the ball with one hand and stomp the foot on the opposite side. He then calls out the side of the hand and the foot. For example, "right hand, left foot."

Letter Chart

F O D C T P V N

B Y E L Z K O A

T E M K B W F H

X B O M S R T F

A R X E P V S D

P M N B C E A O

R C K P E D B G

X F A D R S M P

M T S G O A X U

O H T U K N C S

Pencils With Numbers

Purpose: Ocular Motor

Materials: Type numbers 1-9 on a vertical column on a white piece of paper. Type two columns of the same numbers. Tape these numbers on two pencils. (Figure 1) You will also need a metronome for some of these activities.

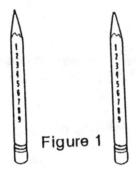

Figure 1

Method: The child is to move his eyes quickly and accurately from one pencil to the other as he holds a pencil in each hand at arm's length. He is to keep his head straight and only move his eyes. For example,

Level 1

1. At your command the child is to move his eyes quickly from the top of one pencil to the other.

2. Have him vary the positions of the pencils. For example, one pencil might be six inches in front of him and the other at arm's length or they may be six inches apart at arm's length or three feet apart at arm's length.

131

Level 2

1. At your command the child is to alternate between the pencils calling out the numbers in sequence from top to bottom. For example, the "1" on the left pencil, then the "1" on the right pencil, "2" on the left pencil, etc.

2. Repeat #1 but vary the positions of the pencils. For example, he can hold the pencils 6 inches apart in front of him or three feet apart. He can hold one pencil 1 foot in front of himself and the other at arm's length.

3. Repeat 1 & 2 but have the child call out the numbers to the beat of a metronome.

Level 3

1. Have the child alternate between pencils by calling out every other number. For example, the "1" on the left pencil, the "2" on the right, the "3" on the left, etc.

2. Repeat #1 but vary the positions of the pencils.

3. Repeat 1 & 2 but use the metronome. Have him call out a number to each beat.

Level 4

1. Have the child alternate between pencils by calling out numbers in sequence starting at the top of one pencil and the bottom of the other. For example, "1" on the left, the "9" on the right, the "2" on the left the "8"on the right, etc.

2. Repeat #1 but vary the position of the pencils and have him call out the numbers to the beat of a metronome.

Near-Far Letter Naming

Purpose: Ocular Motor

Materials: Index cards, blackboard

Method: Type or print some letters or numbers on an index card in several rows. Also print some letters or numbers on several rows on the blackboard. Have the child do this exercise one eye at a time. (Cover one of his eyes) When he can do this exercise without difficulty with one eye at a time, have him do it with both eyes at the same time. Have him seated or standing about 15 feet from the board.

Level 2

1. Hold the index card at about 36 inches in front of his eye. As you slowly move the card towards his eye, he is to call out the letters in a left to right sequence. Stop the card about 6 inches from his eye and quickly remove the card and have him call out the letters on the board in a left to right sequence. Vary the row of letters.

2. Vary #1 by having him call out every other letter or every third letter.

Line Counting

Purpose: Ocular Motor

Materials: Paper, pencil

Method: Draw a series of lines on a sheet of paper. For example,

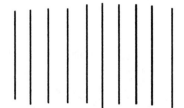

You may want to start with the lines spread out until the child becomes good at this activity.

Level 2

1. Ask the child to touch each line and   count   them in a left to right sequence. See how fast he can count the correct number of lines.

2. Have the child count the lines without touching the paper with his pencil. See how fast he can count the correct number of lines.

Pursuit Reading

Purpose: Ocular Motor

Materials: Reading material to be read for comprehension, walking rail, balance board

Method: Have the child read the material out loud. If he does not know how to read have him spell the words. Always have him spell the words in a left to right sequence.

Level 2

1. Have the child stand and hold the reading material in both hands. Have him move the reading material in circles of varying planes and in other movement patterns, such as "in and out", "right to left", "up and down", and "diagonally".

Level 3

1. Have the child stand and hold the reading material in both hands. Have him move the reading material in circles and other movement patterns such as up and down or left and right as he balances on the balance board or walking rail.

Pencil Pursuits

Purpose: Ocular Motor

Materials: Pencil, finger-puppet

Method: Start by doing the activity one eye at a time (cover one of the child's eyes) and then both eyes at the same time. For younger children use a finger puppet and for older children use a pencil. Have the child seated about 36" in front of you. Slowly move your pencil. He is to follow it with his eyes only. The child is not to move his head or body. Don't use both eyes until he can do each eye individually without any difficulty.

Level 1

1. Have the child follow your pencil with his eyes. You can go left to right, vertically or diagonally. The following are the different patterns you can use. For example,

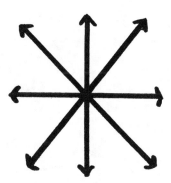

Level 2

1. Have the child follow your pencil with his eyes. Do the same activities as level 1, but also move your pencil in circular patterns. For example, circles or lazy eights.

2. As the child is doing the activities,, ask him questions about his peripheral vision. For example, as you are following the pencil, without taking your eyes off the pencil, how many chairs are at the table?

139

Number Pursuits

Purpose: Ocular Motor

Materials: Metronome, large index cards with up to 12 numbers printed on them.

Method: Start by having the child do this activity with one eye at a time. (Cover his other eye) After he can do this activity easily with one eye, have him use both eyes at the same time. Have him call out the digits in a left to right sequence. He is not to move his head or body, only his eyes. Hold the card about three feet from the child.

Level 2

1. Have him call out the digits in a left to right sequence.

2. As he is calling out the digits, move the card slowly in a circular motion.

Level 3

1. Have him call out the digits in a left to right sequence. Set the metronome to about 60 beats per minute. Each time he hears a beat he calls out a digit.

2. Same as #1 but move the card slowly in a circular motion.

Yardstick Fixations

Purpose: Ocular Motor

Materials: Wooden yardstick, colored map pins

Method: Have the child sitting opposite you at a table.   Hold the yardstick about 2' in front of him as he faces the 18" mark. The yardstick will have colored map pins put at various places on it.   For example,

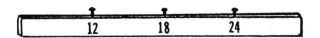

The child will move his eyes quickly from one pin to another in a left to right sequence.   Make sure he moves only his eyes. There should not be any head or body movement.   Start by having the child do these activities one eye at a time.   (Cover one of his eyes)   After he can do each eye individually without any difficulty, have him use both eyes.

Level 1

1. Put the pins at each end and at 12" and 24".   Have the child move his eyes quickly and accurately from one pin to another in a left to right sequence.

2. Vary the location of the pins.

Level 2

1. Put the pins in various locations on the yardstick.   At the beat of the metronome he is to move his eyes quickly and accurately in a left to right sequence from one pin to another.

2. Vary the position of the yardstick.   For example, hold it slightly off center to the right or left, or hold it slightly up or down.   He is still to keep his head straight ahead and only move his eyes.

143

SECTION IV

LATERALITY THERAPY PROCEDURES

Head Roll

Purpose: Laterality

Materials: Metronome for Level 2

Method: Lie the child down on his back, legs together, arms at his side. Have the child look at an object on the ceiling directly above his head. Children under six are too young to have a good understanding of their "right" and "left". If the child is younger than six, help him by showing him which direction "right" is and which direction "left" is throughout the activity.

Observations: Make sure the child leads with his eyes as he turns his head.

Level 1

1. At your command he is to turn his head to the right and look at an object on his right. Next, at your command he turns his head back to the object on the ceiling, and finally, on command, to an object on his left. For example, you call out right and he turns his head to the right and then back to looking at an object on the ceiling.

Level 2

1. Set the metronome to about 40 beats per minute. At each beat, he is to change head position, first to the right then back to the ceiling and finally to the left. He is to call out "right" or "left" as he turns his head. He continues until you tell him to stop. For example, he will say "right", "ceiling", "left", "ceiling", "right", "ceiling", etc.

Body Roll

Purpose: Laterality

Materials: None

Method: Child lies on his back with his legs together and arms at his
side. (Figure 1)

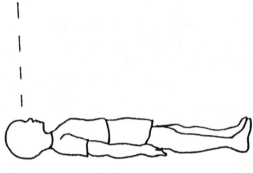

Figure 1

Observations: Make sure he leads with his eyes.

Level 1

1. At your command he is to push off with his left arm and roll completely to
the right until he is again looking straight up at the ceiling. Tell him he is
rolling right. (Figure 2), (Figure 3)

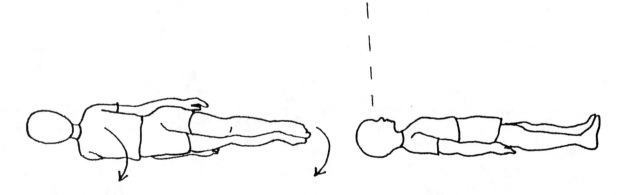

Figure 2   Figure 3

149

2. Do the same as 1 but have him roll to the left as he pushes off with his right arm. Tell him he is rolling left.

Level 2

1. When you clap once have him push off with his left arm and roll completely to his right until he is again looking straight up at the ceiling. He is to call out "right" as he rolls right. When you clap twice he rolls to his left by pushing off with his right arm. He is to call out "left" as he rolls left. Vary your clapping, for example, you may clap for him to go right two times in a row.

Level 3

1. Same as level 2, but tell him to remember the sequence of claps you give him and roll in the proper sequence. For example, clap, clap clap, clap would be roll right, roll left, roll right. Clap, clap, clap clap would be roll right, roll right, roll left. Work up to 5 commands in a roll.

Maze Game

Purpose: Laterality

Materials: Chalkboard

Method: For level 2, draw objects on the blackboard. Make them various sizes and various distances from each other. For example,

On each level the child must get through the maze without hitting an object.

Level 2

1. Have the child stand at one end of the room. Scatter chairs or other objects around the room. The child closes his eyes and starts to walk through the maze. You help him by calling out "left" or "right" as he nears an obstacle.

2. Repeat number one but see if he can remember where the obstacles are. Don't help him by calling out "left" or "right".

Level 3

1. Child puts his chalk at one end of the board. He closes his eyes and tries to get through the maze without hitting any of the objects. You help him by calling out "up", "down", "left" or "right" as he gets near an object.

2. Do both in vertical and horizontal directions. Have him alternate hands.

3. Reduce the number of targets on the board and see if he can remember and get through the maze without you calling out directions.

Level 4

1. Same as level 2 numbers 1 and 2, but the child is to go in the opposite direction from the one you call. For example, if you tell him to go "left", he will have to go "right" to keep from hitting the target. If you say go "up" he will have to go "down".

Decode Chart[72]

Purpose: Laterality

Materials: Decode chart, ball

Method: Hold the chart up in front of the child. Each figure on the chart represents something different for the child to do. For example, the circle can mean "bounce the ball with your left hand", the square "bounce the ball with your right hand", the circle with a face "bounce the ball with both hands", the square with arrows "throw the ball in the air and catch it.

Level 2

1. Only assign commands to two of the figures. For example, the square and the circle. Start at the top and point to these figures. The child is to do what ever you have assigned for each figure as you point to it. Go through the chart in a left to right sequence.

Level 3

1. Only assign commands to three of the figures. Start at the top, point to them and have the child perform the tasks that you have assigned to each one. Go through the chart in a left to right sequence.

Level 4

1. Assign commands to all of the figures. Don't point but have the child start at the top of the chart and work his way to the end doing all of the tasks that you have assigned for the figures.

Decode Chart

Flashlight Walking

Purpose: Laterality

Materials: Two flashlights

Method: Child holds a flashlight in each hand.

Level 3

1. The child is instructed to point the light of the flashlight to either the foot on the same side as his hand holding the flashlight, or the opposite foot as he walks slowly forward. He is to call out the name of the foot which makes the forward movement with the flashlight pointing at it. For example, "left foot". He is then to call out the hand holding the flashlight that is pointing to the forward foot. For example, "left hand". If he was pointing the flashlights to the opposite feet an example of a sequence might be: "left foot" "right hand", "right foot" "left hand", etc.

Walking Procedure[71]

Purpose: Laterality

Materials: Metronome

Method: Have the child do the following activities:

Level 2

1. As the child walks, he calls out, "right hand up", "right leg up", "right hand down", "right leg down". Each time the child says what is to be moved and calls it out as he moves those limbs. He alternates between right and left side as he walks a distance of 10 to 12 feet.

Level 3-A

1. As the child walks, he picks up his leg calling it out. For example, left leg up. Then he lifts up his arm on his other side calling it out. For example, right arm up. He then puts that arm down first, calling it out, then puts the leg down, taking a step and calling it out at the same time.

Level 3-B

1. When the child walks forward, have him call each arm as it moves up and down. For example, "right arm up", "right arm down", "left arm up", "left arm down". When he starts to walk backward, have him call out which leg is moving up and down.

2. Same as #1 but on this procedure set the metronome at 40 beats per minute. Have the child say only one word per beat. For example, on beat one the child would say "right", on beat two, he would say "hand", beat three would be "up". This is a very slow cadence, and for some children it is difficult to stay with the beat.

Level 4

1. Set the metronome to 40 beats per minute. As the child walks forward, he is to say three words per beat. For example, on the first beat, "right arm up", on the second beat "left leg up", on the third beat "left leg down", etc. For children who are unaccustomed to doing things quickly, it may be very difficult for them to say all three words to one beat and move as they say it.

Numbered Circles on Chalkboard

Purpose: Laterality

Materials: Chalkboard, metronome

Method: The numbers one to five are placed randomly on the chalkboard. (As the child becomes good at this the numbers can be increased) The child stands in front of the board. The child circles each number three times. After the third time, he draws a line from number one to number two, circles that three times and then proceeds to each succeeding number.

Level 1

1. Have the child circle each number three times. Have him do it first with his right hand and then with his left.

Level 2

1. Have the child circle all the numbers clockwise or counter clockwise.

2. Have the child circle all even numbers clockwise and all odd numbers counter clockwise.

Level 3

1. Have the child circle all the numbers clockwise or counter clockwise. Numbers are circled to the beat of the metronome starting at the top of the circle on the first beat and the bottom of the circle on the second beat.

2. Use any combination and any number of circles. Letters can be used and have the child spell out words.

Angels In The Snow

Purpose: Laterality

Materials: Marsden ball, metronome

Method: Child lies on his back on the floor with arms along the side of his body and his heels touching. (Figure 1) As you touch or call out one or more of his limbs he moves them out and away from his body.

Figure 1

Observations: Limbs are not to move off the floor, he is to drag them across the floor. Limbs are to reach the end positions at the same time. End position for arms is over his head. (Figure 2) End position for legs is spread out as far as possible. (Figure 3)

Figure 2

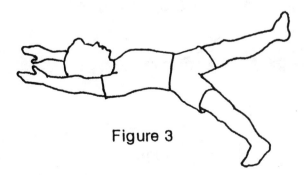

Figure 3

163

Level 1

1. Touch the arm or leg you want him to move. He calls out what he is doing and moves the limb.

2. Repeat 1 but point to the limb to be moved. Don't touch it.

Level 2

1. Child is to move two limbs so that they arrive at the extreme outward position at the same time. For example, both arms over his head, or right arm and right leg, (Figure 4) or right arm and left leg. (Figure 5)

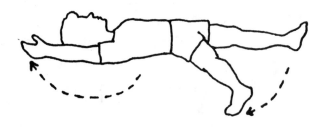

Figure 4

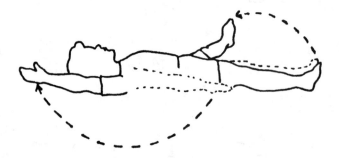

Figure 5

Level 3

1. Set metronome at about 40 beats per minute. Use any arm and leg combination. The limbs are to be moved by a certain number of beats usually starting with four. They are both to arrive at their extreme position at the end of four beats and start their return and arrive at their original position by the end of another four beats.

2. Increase to eight beats.

Level 4

1. With this activity you will use a Marsden Ball. This is a ball about the size of a tennis ball, hanging from the ceiling about three feet over the child's chest. The child is to lie under the Marsden Ball. (Figure 1) Swing the ball in a head to foot direction. Tell the child that when the ball is up toward his head, his right arm and right leg will be out (Figure 2) and when it is at his feet, his left arm and left leg will be out and his right arm and right leg will be back at the starting position.

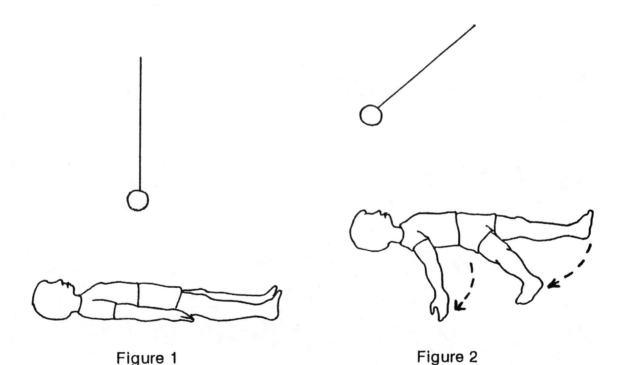

Figure 1   Figure 2

2. Vary the direction of ball and limbs to be moved. For example, swing the ball left to right. When it is at his right, both arms go over his head. When it is at his left, both legs go out and the arms go back to his side.

165

Level 5

1. Set metronome to about 40 beats per minute. Use any leg and arm combination. The limbs are to be moved to a certain number of beats. They are to arrive at their extreme positions at the end of the required number of beats, and return to their original position at the required number of beats. Vary the number of beats per limb. For example, arms over the head in four beats and legs out in eight beats. Use any limb and beat combination.

Coding On Chalkboard[67]

Purpose: Laterality

Materials: Chalkboard

Method: Draw an outline of back and shoulder area with nine circles on it on the chalkboard at child's own height. (Figure 1) When you touch one of the spots on his back he is to point to the corresponding spot on the drawing on the board.

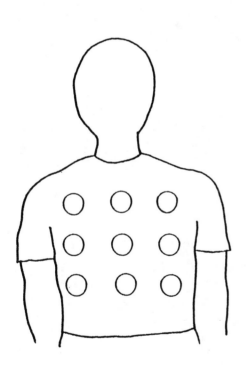
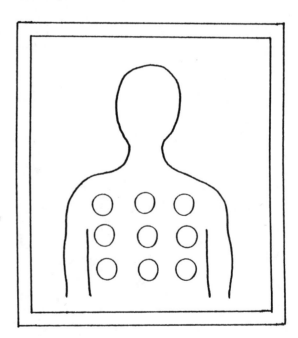

Figure 1

Level 2

1. Touch each of the nine indicated spots on his back until he can locate each one accurately on the projection of his back on the chalkboard before him.

Level 3

1. Tap a pattern from one spot to another rhythmically, starting with two locations and building up to three or more. Repeat in irregular rhythms. He duplicates the pattern on the board.

Level 4

1. Trace a line from one dot to the next on his back. Have him duplicate it on the board. He must draw in the same direction.

Tactile Reinforcement

Purpose: Laterality

Materials: Plastic letters in level 3

Method: Child will follow your directions, with his eyes closed.

Level 2

1. The child has his eyes closed. You touch a part of his body. The child is to tell what part and on what side. For example, right side of face.

2. Child has his eyes closed and his hands on the table. Touch one of his fingers and have him move it. Touch two fingers simultaneously and have him move them.

Level 3-A

1. Child has his eyes closed with his hands in a neutral position. (Figure 1) For example, directly in front of him on a table. You move his hands to a new position for two seconds (Figure 2) and then back to the neutral position.   The child must open his eyes and move his hands to the position you had them. You can use on or both of his hands for this activity.

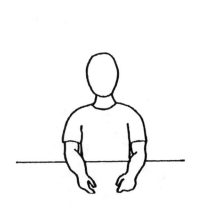

Figure 1

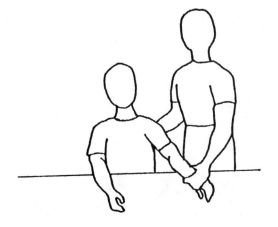

Figure 2

Level 3-B

1. Child has his eyes closed. Put various objects or letters in his hand. Have him tell you what these are with his eyes closed.

Level 4

1. Child has his eyes closed. Draw a simple design on the back of his hand and have him open his eyes and draw it on the board.

The Clock Game[68]

Purpose: Laterality

Materials: Chalkboard

Method: On the chalkboard place eight points equally spaced around the circumference of a circle approximately 18 inches in diameter. For example.

8 1 2

7 [o] 3

6 4

5

The points should be arranged so that one and five determine a vertical axis, points seven and three determine a horizontal axis, and points six and two, eight and four determine two diagonal axes. In the center is a box with an O in the center. The box is the goal for all movement terminating in the center of the circle. In all activities the child should move both hands simultaneously and they should arrive at their respective goals at the same time. Have the child start with each hand on the starting number and move to the stop number. The child should tell you the direction each of his hands will move before he moves them. For example, in activity 2, level 2-A, he will say "I will move my left hand left and my right hand right". (Figure 1 & 2)

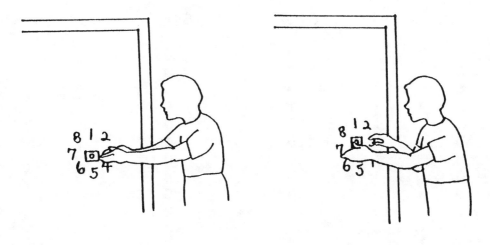

Figure 1   Figure 2

Level 2-A

1. TOWARD THE CENTER. In this activity the child is to start with his two hands on the circumference of the circle and is asked to bring them both toward the center. Use the following order.

LEFT HAND		RIGHT HAND	
START	STOP	START	STOP
7	0	3	0
1	0	5	0
5	0	1	0
8	0	4	0
6	0	2	0

2. OPPOSED MOVEMENT AWAY FROM CENTER

LEFT HAND		RIGHT HAND	
START	STOP	START	STOP
0	7	0	3
0	1	0	5
0	5	0	1
0	8	0	4
0	6	0	2

3. PARALLEL MOVEMENT

LEFT HAND		RIGHT HAND	
START	STOP	START	STOP
7	0	0	3
0	7	3	0
1	0	0	5
0	1	5	0
5	0	0	1
0	5	1	0
8	0	0	4
0	8	4	0
6	0	0	2
0	6	2	0

Level 2-B

1. MOVEMENT WITH CROSS MERIDIANS, MOVEMENT TOWARD CENTER

LEFT HAND		RIGHT HAND	
START	STOP	START	STOP
7	0	1	0
7	0	5	0
1	0	3	0
5	0	3	0
8	0	1	0
8	0	3	0
8	0	5	0
6	0	1	0
6	0	3	0
6	0	5	0
8	0	2	0
6	0	4	0
7	0	2	0
7	0	4	0
1	0	2	0
1	0	4	0
5	0	2	0
5	0	4	0

2. MOVEMENT AWAY FROM CENTER

LEFT HAND		RIGHT HAND	
START	STOP	START	STOP
0	7	0	2
0	7	0	5
0	1	0	3
0	5	0	3
0	8	0	1
0	8	0	3
0	8	0	5
0	6	0	1
0	6	0	3
0	6	0	5
0	8	0	2
0	6	0	4
0	7	0	2
0	7	0	4
0	1	0	2
0	1	0	4
0	5	0	2
0	5	0	4

Level 3

1. CROSS MOVEMENT - CROSS MERIDIAN, MOVEMENT LEFT TO RIGHT

LEFT HAND		RIGHT HAND	
START	STOP	START	STOP
7	0	0	1
7	0	0	5
7	0	0	2
7	0	0	4
8	0	0	3
8	0	0	5
8	0	0	1
8	0	0	2
6	0	0	3
6	0	0	1
6	0	0	4
6	0	0	5

2. MOVEMENT TO LEFT, CROSS MOVEMENT

LEFT HAND		RIGHT HAND	
START	STOP	START	STOP
0	7	1	0
0	7	5	0
0	7	2	0
0	7	4	0
0	8	3	0
0	8	5	0
0	8	1	0
0	8	2	0
0	6	3	0
0	6	1	0
0	6	4	0
0	6	5	0

Midline Training

Purpose: Laterality

Materials: Penlight

Method: Follow the directions in each section. Explain what a midline is and show the child both his midline and your midline. (Figure 1)

Figure 1

Level 1

1. Have the child hold his arms straight out in front of him. Have him move his arms out all the way to his sides and back to the starting point. Each time his arms move out he is to say, "out". Each time his arms move in he is to say, "in". Repeat with his eyes closed.

Level 2

1. Have him hold his right arm pointing to the right as he faces straight ahead. Have him move his arm towards his midline and call out "out-in" as he does it. Have him stop at his midline, continue from the midline calling out "in-out" until his right arm is pointing all the way to his left. (Figure 2) Repeat this with his left arm going from left to right. Do this with his eyes opened and closed.

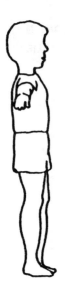  

Figure 2

Level 3-A

1. Have him hold his right arm pointing to the right as he faces straight ahead. Have him move his arm towards his midline and call out "right to left" and stop at his midline. As he continues from midline, he again calls out "left". Do the same thing with his arm going from left to right.

2. Repeat #1 but with his right arm pointing all the way to the left and going from left to right and have him call out "left to right". Do the same with his left arm pointing to the right and going from right to left.

3. Do both 1 & 2 again but don't stop at the midline. Make a continuous motion going from either right to left or left to right. Do with eyes opened and closed.

Level 3-B

1. Darken the room and have the child seated in a chair. Stand across the room with a penlight. Start on his right side and have him call out "right to left" as it approaches his midline and again "right to left" as it crosses his midline. Do the same thing starting on his left side.

Reciprocal Movements[69]

Purpose: Laterality

Materials: None

Method: The child is to imitate your movements.

Level 1

1. Have the child stand in front of you with his hands in front of him at chest level. Have him open one of his hands while he closes the other. This can also be done to a metronome.

2. With his arms out at his side, at shoulder level, (Figure 1) have him move one arm up while the other moves down.

3. Have him move one arm up and the leg on the opposite side out. (Figure 2)

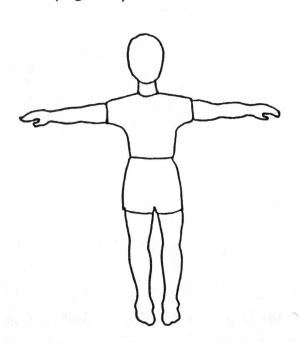

Figure 1

Figure 2

Level 2

1. Stand in front of the child with your arms out at the side at shoulder level and have him move the same side as you do. For example, you move your right arm up and he moves his left arm up.

2. Stand in front of the child. Have him move the same limb as you, as if he were facing in your direction. For example, you move your left arm up, he moves his left arm up. (Figure 3)

Figure 3

Level 3

1. Stand in front of the child with both of your arms out at the side at shoulder level. Have him move the same limb as you as he would if he was facing in your direction but have him move it in the opposite direction that you do. For example, you move your right arm up, he moves his right arm down, you move your arm in towards your body, he moves his out.

180

Level 4

1. Stand next to the child with both arms out at the side at shoulder level. (Figure 4) The child must imitate in reverse with one side of his body these movements imposed by you on the other side of his body. For example, you move your right arm up as he moves his left arm down. Start next to the child. (Figure 5) Move later to face him.

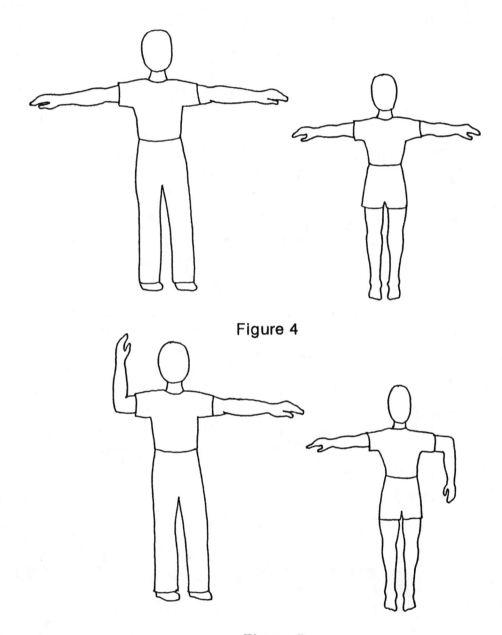

Figure 4

Figure 5

Tic-Tac-Toe

Purpose: Laterality

Materials: Blackboard

Method: You will play tic-tac-toe with the child using the blackboard.

Level 2

a. The child must call out the square he wants to put his "X" in. For example, "top left".

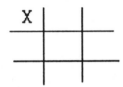

b. He puts his X in the square, you then put your "O" in the square you want.

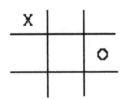

c. The child only gets one chance at naming the correct square. If he calls out "top right", that's the square the "X" goes in.

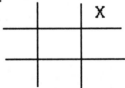

Level 3

1. Child must call out the square he wants to put his "X" in. For example, "top left". For this activity he does not mark it on the board. He must remember where he put the "X". You can put your "O's" on the board but he must remember where he put his X's.

X's Procedure[74]

Purpose: Laterality

Materials: Chalkboard, metronome

Method: Place seven X's on the chalkboard with the center X at nose height. The side X's are 12 to 18 inches from the center X (the distance is dependent on the child's size). Two other X's are placed one directly above and one directly below the side X's. Have the child hold a piece of chalk in each hand.

```
        X           X

        X     X     X

        X           X
```

Figure 1

The child starts by placing the chalk on the X's you tell him and he follows your directions as to what directions you want him to move each hand. Each hand always goes from the starting X to the designated X and then back to the starting X.

Level 2 Have the child do the following:

1. The right hand chalk is placed on the right X and the left hand chalk on the left X. Tell the child to look at the center X. Then move each chalk to the center X and back to the starting place, one at a time, as he calls out which hand he is going to move.

2. Tell him to move his right hand first then his left hand and then both hands saying "right", "left", "both" as he does it. This results in his right hand going to the center and his left hand going to the center and then both hands going back to their starting places.

3. Another variation of this is "right, both, left". When he says "right" the right hand goes from right to center; on "both" the left hand goes from left to center and the right hand from center to right; and on "left" the left hand goes from center to left.

Level 3

1. The child is instructed to move his chalk from any X to any other X. For example, the right hand can go from the right X to the top right X while the left hand goes from the left side X to the bottom left X. For example, a command of right, left, both would be moving the right chalk to the top right X, moving the left chalk to the lower left X, and moving both hands back to the starting points.

2. Use the metronome. He does one movement to each beat.

3. Increase the directions to four then five. For example, four directions can be "right, both, left, both".

4. Place the X's in different positions. The three horizontal X's remain in the same position, but the vertical X's are changed.

Arrows On Board

Purpose: Laterality

Materials: Chalkboard, metronome

Method: Draw four arrows on the board. Draw one up, one down, one to the right and one to the left. The child is to stand about 10 feet in front of them. For example,

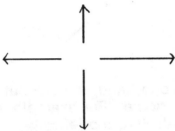

Each time he hears the metronome, he moves his hands to another arrow and calls out the direction it is pointing. Work clockwise or counter clockwise.

Level 2

1. Child stands in front of the arrows. Each time he hears the metronome he holds his hands together and points them in the direction the arrows are pointing and calls out the direction. Start with the top arrow and work clockwise or counter clockwise. For example,

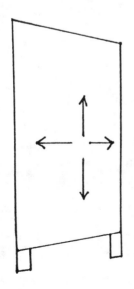 

187

Level 3

1. This time he points with both hands held together when the arrows are pointing up or down and with his right hand for the right arrow and his left hand for the left arrow.

Level 4

1. Add four more arrows. For example,

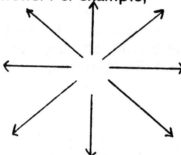

Have the child just use one hand and call out the directions of the arrows at the beat of the metronome. For example, top, top right, right, bottom right, bottom, bottom left, left, top left.

2. Vary this by having him point with both hands held together for the top and bottom arrows and the right hand for the right arrows and the left hand for the left arrows.

Vertical Lines

Purpose: Laterality

Materials: Visual motor activity sheet, metronome

Method: Child is seated at a table with you next to him. He is to hold the activity sheet at normal reading distance. At the beat of the metronome, he calls out the position of the vertical line to the horizontal line. For example, the top row going left to right would be right up, middle down, right down, left up.

Level 3

1. Have him do each row in a left to right direction, calling out the positions.

2. Have him go in a vertical direction.

3. Without the metronome, time him in both the horizontal and vertical directions. Record his speed.

Visual Motor Activity Sheet

Body Awareness

Purpose: Laterality

Materials: None

Method: Have the child do the following:

Level 1

Have the child sit on the floor, knees bent, feet flat on the floor. Tell him to do the following:

1. Put your left hand on your right toe.
2. Clap your hands twice.
3. Put your left hand on your left toe.
4. Put your elbows together.
5. Touch your heels.
6. Touch your eyes.
7. Put your feet apart.
8. Touch one elbow.
9. Touch two elbows.
10. Draw a square in the air.
11. Clap one time.
12. Clasp your hands behind your neck.
13. Touch one shoulder.
14. Put your knees together.
15. Touch your right knee with your left hand.
16. Touch your left knee with your right hand.
17. Place your palms together.
18. Clap your hands twice.
19. Touch one knee and one foot.
20. Put your hands on your head.
21. Touch your nose.
22. Touch your toes with your arms crossed.
23. Touch your nose with one hand, your knee with the other.
24. Put your right hand on your left knee.
25. Cross your arms in front of your chest.
26. Put your right hand over your left eye.
27. Cross your arms in front of your chest.
28. Put your left hand on your right knee.
30. Put your right hand on your left hip.
31. Cross your arms in front of your chest.

193

32. Put your left hand on your right hip.
33. Cross your arms in front of your chest.
34. Put your left hand on your right foot.
35. Cross your arms in front of your chest.
36. Put your right hand on your left foot.
37. Cross your arms in front of your chest.
38. Put your left hand on your right ear.
39. Cross your arms in front of your chest.
40. Put your right hand on your left ear.
41. Cross your arms in front of your chest.

Laterality Coding

Purpose: Laterality

Materials: Blackboard or paper, laterality coding chart

Method: The following symbols are used in this activity.

O = Hand   △ = Foot

Left Hand = O | Right Hand = | O

Left Foot = △ | Right Foot = | △

Both Hands = φ   Both Feet = ▲

Right Foot and Right Hand = | △ O

Left Foot and Left Hand = △ O |

Use the Laterality Coding Chart and as you point to each symbol the child will either raise his hand or stomp the appropriate foot. He should also call out which hand or foot he is using. For example, left foot, right hand, etc.

Level 3

1. Go through the chart in a left to right direction. Then go through the chart in a top to bottom direction.

Laterality Coding Chart

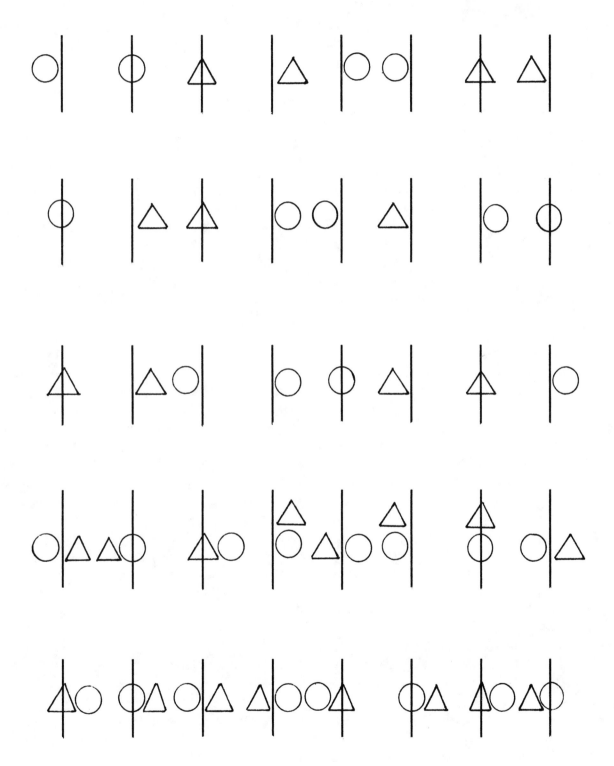

SECTION V

DIRECTIONALITY THERAPY PROCEDURES

Letter Orientation

Purpose: Directionality

Materials: Chalkboard, magazine pictures

Method: Child will do the following activities.

Level 1

1. Cut pictures from a magazine and turn them in different directions. Ask the child if they are backwards or not. Ask him if it makes a difference for the identification of the picture if it is backwards or not. Show him the orientation of letters and show him how their orientation is important for identification but not pictures.

Level 2

1. Draw letters or numbers on the blackboard. Have some facing in the wrong direction. Have him circle the ones that are wrong and have him draw them the proper way.

Level 3

1. Have the child circle certain letters in a line of print from a magazine. For example, all the b's or d's.

Level 4

1. Draw some letters on the board. Ask him to draw the letter as it would look if it was turned 1/2 to the right or left, upside down, etc.

b-d-p-q Sorting

Purpose: Directionality

Materials: b-d-p-q Sorting Worksheets, metronome, balance disc or walking rail

Method: Place the b-d-p-q sorting chart at eye level on the wall.

Level 2

1. Child stands in front of the chart and touches each letter as he calls it out, going from left to right or top to bottom.

Level 3

1. Child stands in front of the chart and names each letter to the beat of the metronome.

2. Have the child touch and name any one letter. For example, all b's or all d's. Do to the beat of the metronome.

3. Do #2. First with right hand and then with the left hand.

4. Alternate hands. Touch the first letter with his right hand and call it out, then touch the second letter with his left hand and call it out.

Level 4

1. Child stands on balance disc or end of walking rail in front of chart. He is to call out the sounds the letters make instead of the names of the letters. For example, the "buh" sound or "duh" sound or "puh" sound.

2. Call out the names of every other letter or every third letter. Do in both vertical and horizontal directions.

3. Go left to right and call out the name of the letter and say the direction the loop is facing. For example, q "left", b "right".

b-d-p-q Sorting Chart

q   b   p   d   b   p   q

d   p   d   q   p   d   p

p   d   p   b   d   b   d

d   p   q   d   b   d   p

b   d   p   q   d   p   b

p   b   d   p   b   p   d

b   p   b   d   p   q   p

p   d   q   p   b   d   b

q   b   d   b   d   q   d

Directional "U" Saccades

Purpose: Directionality

Materials: Directional "U", Worksheet

Method: Set the metronome at 60 beats per minute. (slower or faster if desired) The child stands 20 feet away from the worksheet which is hung on the wall.

Level 1

1. Tell the child to clasp his hands together and extend them in front of himself. To each beat of the metronome he is to move his hands in the direction of the opening in each "U". Do each line in a left to right manner.

Level 2

1. Tell the child to clasp his hands together and extend them in front of himself. To each beat of the metronome he is to move his hands in the direction of the opening of each "U" and call out the directions. (right, left, up, or down) Do each line in a left to right manner.

2. Repeat #1 going down the vertical columns from top to bottom.

3. Without the metronome and without using his hands see how fast he can do both the horizontal and vertical rows and call out the direction of each opening.

Directional "U"

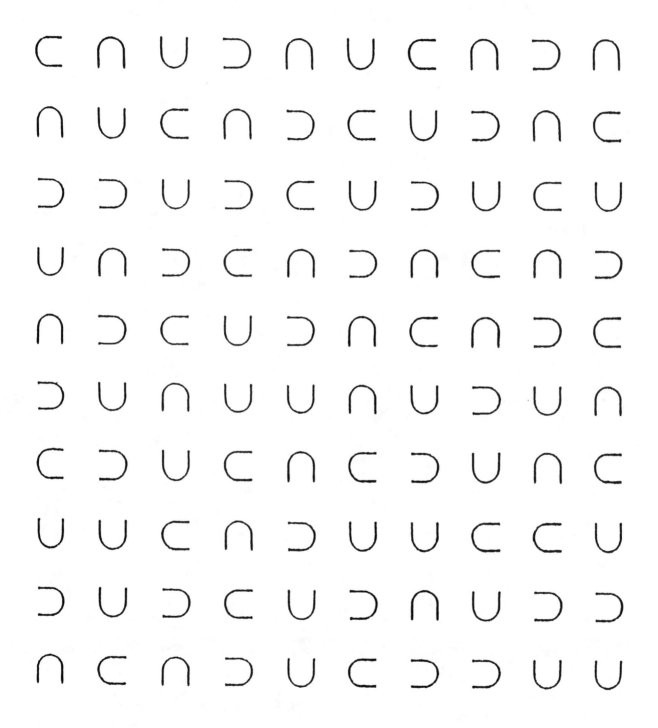

Directional Arrows

Purpose: Directionality

Materials: Metronome, directional arrows worksheet

Method: The child is seated at a table with you sitting next to him. Have him hold the worksheet at normal reading distance.

Level 2

1. At the beat of the metronome the child is to name the direction of each arrow. Start on the horizontal line and move in a left to right sequence.

2. Same as #1 but go down the vertical lines from top to bottom.

3. Without the metronome, time him and see how fast he can do the horizontal and vertical lines.

Level 3

1. At the beat of the metronome the child is to walk in a heel to toe manner on the walking rail. As he walks, have him call out the direction of the arrows. Go in both the horizontal direction and the vertical direction.

Directional Arrows

↓ → ↓ ↓ ← ↑

→ ← → ↑ ↑ ←

→ → ↑ → ↓ ←

↓ ← ← ↑ ↓ →

← ← → ↑ ← ↓

← → ↑ → ↓ ↓

↓ → ↓ ↓ ← ↑

→ ← → ↑ ↑ ←

Teach Letters By Classes

Purpose: Directionality

Materials: Blackboard

Method: On the blackboard show the child all the letters in the alphabet by classes. For example, all the letters with loops to the right, loops to the left, letters with horizontal lines, vertical lines, lines that cross, and curved lines.

Level 1

1. Have the child practice drawing all the letters of the alphabet on the blackboard by classes.

Level 2

1. Tell the child which class of letters you want him to find and have him circle them on a book or magazine.

Flash Cards and Reversed Letters

Purpose: Directionality

Materials: 3"x 5" index cards

Method: Print in lower case letters, words from the child's Instant Words List (pgs. 219-220) on the index cards. Print one word per card. Purposely reverse letters in about half of the words. Have the remaining words correct with no letters reversed.

Level 2

1. Give the child the flash cards one at a time. He is to study the card and tell you whether the card has an error or not. If it does contain an error, he circles it and then writes the word correctly on a chalkboard or piece of paper.

2. Flash each card to the child for about three seconds. Have him tell you if any of the letters were reversed or not. Have him correctly print any word that had a letter reversed in it.

INSTANT WORDS[76]

These are the words most used in reading and writing English, grouped in order of frequency of use.

1	2	3	4	5	6
the	he	go	who	saw	big
a	I	see	an	home	where
is	they	then	their	soon	am
you	one	us	she	stand	ball
to	good	no	new	box	morning
and	me	him	said	upon	live
we	about	by	did	first	four
that	had	was	boy	came	last
in	if	come	three	girl	color
not	some	get	down	house	away
for	up	or	work	find	red
at	her	two	put	because	friend
with	do	man	were	made	pretty
it	when	little	before	could	eat
on	so	has	just	book	want
can	my	them	long	look	year
will	very	how	here	mother	white
are	all	like	other	run	got
of	would	our	old	school	play
this	any	what	take	people	found
your	been	know	cat	night	left
as	out	make	again	into	men
but	there	which	give	say	bring
be	from	much	after	think	wish
have	day	his	many	back	black

7	8	9	10	11	12
may	ran	ask	hat	off	fire
let	five	small	car	sister	ten
use	read	yellow	write	happy	order
these	over	show	try	once	part
right	such	goes	myself	didn't	early
present	way	clean	longer	set	fat
tell	too	buy	those	round	third
next	shall	thank	hold	dress	same
please	own	sleep	full	fall	love
leave	most	letter	carry	wash	hear
hand	sure	jump	eight	start	yesterday
more	thing	help	sing	always	eyes
why	only	fly	warm	anything	door
better	near	don't	sit	around	clothes
under	than	fast	dog	close	though
while	open	cold	ride	walk	o'clock
should	kind	today	hot	money	second
never	must	does	grow	turn	water
each	high	face	cut	might	town
best	far	green	seven	hard	took
another	both	every	woman	along	pair
seem	end	brown	funny	bed	now
tree	also	coat	yes	fine	keep
name	until	six	ate	sat	head
dear	call	gave	stop	hope	food

Fill in the Loops

Purpose: Directionality

Materials: Book or magazine, red pen, blue pen

Method: Do the following activities.

Level 3

1. Use a page from a book or magazine. The child is to fill in all the loops of letters facing the right with red and all the loops of letters facing left with blue.

2. Time him. See how fast he can complete a page without missing any loops.

Level 4

1. Use a page from a book or magazine. The child is to fill in all the loops of letters facing the right in red and facing left in blue.

2. Once the child can do #1, instead of filling in the loops he is to call out the letter and which color he would have used to fill in the loop.

The Bed

Purpose: Directionality

Materials: None

Method: Explain to the child that the loop on the "b" faces to the right. Hold his left hand in front of him with his thumb pointing to the right. For example,

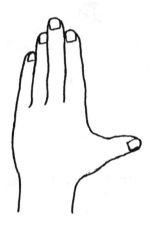

Explain how the loop on the "d" faces to the left. Hold his left hand in front of him with his thumb pointing to the left. For example,

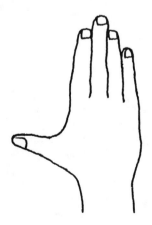

Level 2

1. A good way for the child to remember the direction of the b and d is to have him hold his two hands together to form a bed. Have him practice spelling "bed". For example,

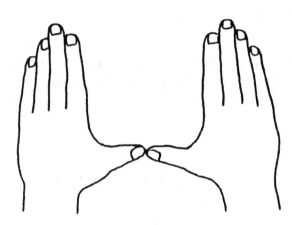

The left hand with the thumb pointing to the right is the "b", the right hand with the thumb pointing to the left is the "d".

Vectors

Purpose: Directionality

Materials: Blackboard, protractor

Method: A vector is a straight line drawn at different angles. For example,

On the board draw several vectors. Show the child how the angle can change between the vector and the straight horizontal line.

Level 2

1. On the blackboard draw a vector. Have the child draw one like yours next to it on the board. It must be close to the same angle as the one you have drawn. Draw several in different positions for the child to copy.

Level 3

1. Make large letters on the board. Show the child how vectors can be part of a letter. For example,

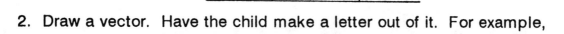

2. Draw a vector. Have the child make a letter out of it. For example,

 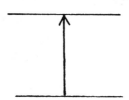

Level 4

1. Make a vector on a piece of paper. Let the child look at it for a few seconds and then have the child draw the same one on the blackboard.

Level 5

1. Draw a vector on a piece of paper with a protractor. Have the child make one just like it with his protractor.

2. Draw a vector on the paper with the protractor. The child must make a vector with the same angle but in the opposite direction. For example,

Commonly Reversed[75] Words

Purpose: Directionality

Materials: 3 x 5 index cards, blackboard

Method: The following are commonly reversed words: on, no, saw, was, not, ton, dam, mad, rat, tar, pot, top, bat, tab, wed, dew, mug, gum, pit, tip.

Level 4-A

1. Have the child make cards with commonly reversed words. Then have the child fingertrace the word while saying it. Next, remove the card and have the child write the word from memory. Repeat this procedure until the child can read and write the word several times without error.

2. Use one of the words in a sentence and have the child indicate the same word on the card.

Level 4-B

1. Make a list of commonly reversed words with one word over the paired reversed word, allowing some space between the two pairs. Then have him draw a line between similar letters. For example,

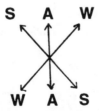

2. On a 3 X 5 index card, print or write one of the commonly reversed words. Purposely miswrite a letter in some of the words. For example, "toq" instead of "top". The child is to tell you whether the word looks right or wrong and why.

227

Distinctive Features

Purpose: Directionality

Materials: Chalkboard, magazine pictures, metronome, plastic or wooden letters

Method: Have the child do the following activities.

Level 1

1. Show the child a picture from a magazine. Ask him questions about the picture. For example, how many cars are in the picture? What color are they? What is the man in the picture wearing?

2. Show the child two different pictures of the same object. For example, cars. Ask him how the two pictures are different.

Level 2-A

1. Draw letters on the chalkboard. Make them large and put numbers next to the letter so that as the child looks at the numbers in sequence he will be scanning the letter in the proper top to bottom or left to right direction. For example,

At each beat of the metronome have him move his eyes to the next number. Train all capital and lower case letters together.

Level 2-B

1. Have the child group the alphabet by classes. For example, all letters with loops, with curves, with diagonal lines, with just vertical and horizontal lines. Make sure he knows what vertical, horizontal and diagonal mean. Have him draw the letters on the blackboard.

Level 3-A

1. Draw part of a letter on the board. Have the child tell you what letter it is. When you do this, use mainly horizontal and vertical lines as these are the lines that give us the most information for letter recognition.

2. In a line of letters from a book have him circle all the letters with vertical, horizontal or diagonal lines.

3. Show the child a picture from a magazine. Have him find an many angles, curves, horizontal, vertical and diagonal lines as possible. Ask him what letters these could make.

Level 3-B

1. Have the child describe how one letter is different from another.

2. When a child draws a letter, have him verbally describe it. For example, as he draws a "b" he describes the vertical line and the loop that is attached to the lower right side.

Level 3-C

1. Letter counting: on a line of letters from a book, have the child count how many of certain letters there are, for example, how many b's or d's, etc.

2. With his eyes closed have the child feel upper and lower case plastic or wooden letters and tell you which letter he is feeling. Have him describe the letter.

Level 4-A

1. Write some letters on the chalkboard. Ask him which letter does not belong in the group. For example; N, W, K, P - the answer would be P because it is the only letter with a loop.

Level 4-B

1. Have the child find as many different styles of print as he can. Ask him how the letters are different for each style. Ask him how they are the same.

2.   Have the child look at the page of a book. Have him describe how certain words are shaped alike. For example, same length, start with the same letter, have a lot of letters with loops, etc.

Level 5

1.   Ask him how many ways he can describe the parts of a letter. For example, b could be described: vertical line, curved line, closed loop at bottom of the letter, vertical line to the left of the loop. The letter N could be described: two vertical lines, one vertical line to the left of the diagonal, one vertical line to the right of the diagonal, two small angles, where the lines intersect, the diagonal line touches the top of the left vertical line and the bottom of the right vertical line.

Colored Rulers[64]

Purpose: Directionality

Materials: Colored cardboard rulers, 1" by 6" cut from cardboard paper, paper and a pencil

Method: This activity is to help eliminate the reversal of letters when printing. The child will make the first stroke of the letter by using the ruler. The first stroke will be made on the side that has the capital letter printed on it. For example,

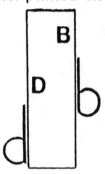

Make a ruler for the following letters:

Level 2

1. You spell the word for the child and then have the child use the ruler to print the following words: bee, boy, bat, bin, ball, dog, doll, dig, dam, ding.

    b. Think up other words that can be used with the ruler.
    c. Once the child is able to print words using the ruler, have him try it without the ruler.

Bilateral Circles[73]

Purpose: Directionality

Materials: Chalkboard, metronome

Method: An "X" is placed at nose height in front of the child on a blackboard. The child stands and looks at the "X" while being visually and physically aware of what his arms and hands are doing as he moves his arms to draw large circles on the blackboard. The circles should be about twelve inches in diameter.

Level 1

1. Have the child stand in front of the blackboard and look at the "X". The "X" should be at nose level directly in front of him. Have the child practice drawing circles one level at a time. He should try and make the circles as round as possible and stay on the same line. Have him do it first with his right hand and then his left.

Level 2

1. The child's first task is to figure out the four different combinations of directions the arms can move while making two circles simultaneously. He is helped as little as possible in figuring this out. The goal is to have him be able to work out the logic that the hands can go different ways: two ways in the same direction and two ways in the opposite direction. For example,

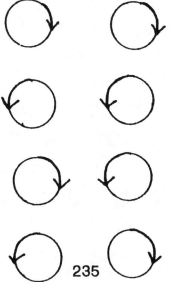

235

2. Practice having him draw the two circles at the same time. Practice having him move his arms in the four different directions. Try and have him make the circles as close to the same size as possible.

Level 3

1. Draw a vertical line at the top and at the bottom of each circle.

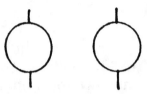

As he draws around the circles and the chalk comes to the top line, he is to say "top" and when it comes to the bottom line, he is to say "bottom".

2. The metronome is added. On the first beat he should have the chalk at the top line and say "top", on the second beat he should have moved the chalk at a speed that will have it at the bottom line and he says "bottom".

3. Same activities as 1 & 2 but one circle may be higher or lower or larger or smaller than the other.

Level 4

1. Two circles are placed on the board in front of the child. Two lines are placed vertically and horizontally. Use the metronome. For example,

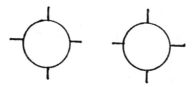

The child makes circles in each of the four different directions his arms can move. (Two in the same direction and two in the opposite direction.) As he comes to each line, at the beat of the metronome, he says the position of the chalk so that in addition to "top" and "bottom", he says "right" and "left" when both hands are on the sides of the circles. When the hands are going in the opposite direction he says "in" and "out" instead of "right" and "left".

Level 5

1. The procedure involves one circle with four lines dividing it into quarters and one with three lines dividing it into thirds. The circles are about twelve inches in diameter. For example,

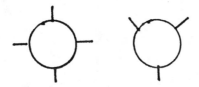

The childs hands go around the circles in the four different directions; two in the same direction and two in the opposite direction. Each hand is to reach the next line on the next beat of the metronome. One hand must travel faster than the other to attain accuracy. No words are to be said as he completes this procedure. One hand traces the circle in four beats while the other is doing it in three beats. These circles can also be made in different sizes as well as different heights on the board.

Chalkboard Squares

Purpose: Directionality

Materials: Chalkboard, metronome

Method: An "X" is placed at nose height on the board in front of the child. Two squares about 12 inches in size are placed on either side of the X. For example,

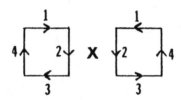

Level 1

1. Have the child stand in front of the "X" with the "X" at nose level. Have him practice tracing the squares. Have him trace the right square with his right hand and the left square with his left. He is to try and stay on the lines.

Level 2

1. Have the child start in the same corner of each square. Make both hands follow the lines to each corner of the squares, first in one direction and then in the opposite direction.

2. Have him do #1 but call out the direction in which his hands are going.

Level 3

1. Have the left hand start at the top left corner of the left square, and the right hand at the top right corner of the right square. The instructions are "make your hands go in two different directions, calling out the directions the hands are going as you move them." The right hand will go from right to left and the left hand from left to right. The child would say "in, down, out, and up". The next direction would be both hands going "down" and then in toward each other, saying, "in, up, out". This gives four different directions for tracing squares. For example,

2. Do same as #1 but a metronome is set at 40 beats. The child is told to be at a corner each time the metronome beats, and say the direction that the hands move.

Level 4

1. Have the child put both hands at the top left corner of each square and go in opposite directions. This is done at the beat of the metronome (40 beats a minute) but without saying the direction in which the hands are going. For instance, starting at the top left of both squares the right hand goes right and the left down. On the next beat, the right hand goes down and the left right.

2. Same as #1 but make squares of different sizes and heights on the board.

Figure Eights

Purpose: Directionality

Materials: Chalkboard, metronome

Method: Two eights at 12 inches apart and about two feet tall are placed at each side of an X drawn at nose height. On the blackboard a vertical line is drawn at the top and bottom of both eights and a horizontal line through the middle of the eights. For example,

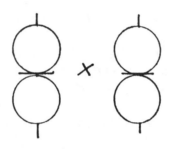

Level 1.

1. Have the child stand in front of the "X" when it is at nose level. He is to trace the right figure eight with his right hand and the left with his left hand. He is to try and stay on the lines.

Level 2

1. The child stands and looks at the X. He is to figure out the four different combinations of directions the arms can move while tracing the two eights simultaneously. For example,

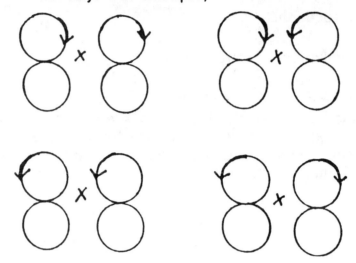

2. Same as #1 but use the metronome and have the child call out the directions his hands are moving. For example: "top", "middle" and "bottom" as he crosses the lines on each beat of the metronome.

3. Make the eights different sizes and do the same as #2.

Level 3

1. Draw the eights on their sides. (lazy eights) For example,

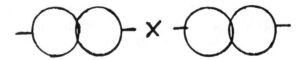

A metronome is used while the child calls out the direction his hands move. For example, if both his hands start at the left line and move up he will call out "top", "middle", "bottom", "side".

2. Set the metronome at a slow beat. At each beat he is to be at the horizontal lines. He doesn't have to call out directions.

3. Vary the locations the hands start from. For example, one hand can start on the left side of the left figure eight and the other hand can start on the right side of the right figure eight. Use the metronome at a slow rate.

Triangle & Square

Purpose: Directionality

Materials: Chalkboard, metronome

Method: Put an "X" on the board at nose height in front of the child. Draw a square and a traingle on either side of the "X". The square and triangle are about one foot in height. For example,

Level 3

1. Have the   child trace the lines of each figure simultaneously.   The metronome is used but the child is not to name the direction of the hands, because one hand makes three different directional movements to complete   the task and the other makes four. Have the child figure out the four different directions that the two figures can be traced.

SECTION VI

SEQUENTIAL PROCESSING THERAPY PROCEDURES

Clock Memory Game

Purpose: Sequential Processing

Materials: Chalkboard

Method: Have the child stand in front of the chalkboard looking at a target at nose level. Place eight numbers in a 12" to 18" diameter around the center target like the numbers on a clock. For example,

$$8 \quad 1 \quad 2$$
$$7 \quad \times \quad 3$$
$$6 \quad 5 \quad 4$$

Level 1

1. Have him look at the numbers and then close his eyes. See how many he can remember and point to with his eyes closed as you call them out one number at a time.

Level 2

1. Same as level 1, but call the numbers out in sequence, for example, 2,6,7. The child must remember and point to them in the proper sequence.

2. Same as #1, but use letters instead of numbers.

Auditory Span

Purpose: Sequential Processing

Materials: Pencil and paper

Method: Have the child seated at a table. For children 5 and under don't use more than 4 numbers, for older children don't use more than 7 numbers.

Level 1

1. Call out numbers in a row and have the child repeat them back to you. For example: 5,7,6,8.

Level 2

1. Call out numbers in a row and have the child close his eyes for a few seconds, visualize them, then repeat them back to you.

2. Same as number 1, but if he is old enough, have him write the numbers down after he says them.

Level 3

1. Call out numbers in a row and have the child repeat them and write them down. However, you are going to tell him to leave one of the numbers out. For example, call out, "4,7,8,9,6". Tell the child to say the numbers and write them down, but to leave out the 7. The child would say and write 4,8,9,6.

Level 4

1. For this, don't use more than 5 numbers and start with only 3. When he can do 3, go to 4, then 5 numbers. Call out numbers in a row and tell him to leave one number out and then write them backwards. For example, 4,7,6,5 leave out the 6. He would write 5,7,4.

Color Sequencing

Purpose: Sequential Processing

Materials: Colored pens

Method: Draw some colored circles in a row. For example, red, blue, yellow, green. Show the child the circles for a few seconds and then hide them from his view.

Level 1

1. Draw no more than three circles. Show them to the child for a few seconds. Have him tell you the colors in the proper sequence.

Level 2

1. Draw no more than four circles. Show them to the child for a few seconds. Have him tell you the colors in sequence.

2. Have him tell you the colors in reverse sequence.

Level 3

1. Draw up to seven circles in a row. Have the child tell you the colors in proper sequence or in reverse sequence.

2. Have him tell you the proper sequence but he is to leave one of the colors out. For example, red, blue, red, yellow, green. Have him repeat the proper sequence but leave out the red. For example, blue, yellow, green.

Level 4

1. Draw up to seven circles. Have him write the names of the colors in sequence on paper instead of calling them out.

2. Have him substitute one color for another. For example, every time he sees blue he will substitute red for it.

Level 5

1. Draw up to seven circles. Put labels on the colors. For example, a red circle will be called "A" or a blue circle will be called "B" or a green circle will be called "T". He is to write the labels in proper sequence instead of the color names. For example, green, red and blue will be "T,A,B".

2. Spell out words with the colors. For example, using the labels in #1 BAT would be blue, red, green. See if he can figure out the word.

Sequence Memory Skills

Purpose: Sequential Processing

Materials: Various objects in the room, metronome

Method: Assign letters or numbers to different objects in the room. For example, the chair is number 1, the table is number 2, the lamp is number 3, etc.

Level 1

1. After you call out a sequence, have the child run and touch the objects in sequence. Do not do more than 4 at a time.

Level 2

1. After you call out a sequence, have the child run to and touch the objects in sequence. Work up to 5 or more objects.

2. Vary this by having him run out of sequence, for example, 4,2,1,3.

Level 3

1. Label parts of his body with numbers. For example, #1 is his right arm, #2 is his left foot, etc. Have him move the parts in sequence. For example, #1 right arm, #2 left foot, #3 right foot, #4 left hand. You call out a number sequence. He then moves and calls out those body parts in that sequence.

2. Do to beat of a metronome.

Level 4

1. Label parts of the child's body with numbers. Label parts of your body with letters. For example, you label his right arm #1, left leg #2, head #3, your right leg "A", left arm "B" and your head "C". You call out a sequence and he then points to and calls out the proper sequence of body parts. For example, 2,3,B would be his left leg, head and your left arm.

Rhythm[70]

Purpose: Sequential Processing

Materials: Metronome

Method: Child is to reproduce the rhythm pattern. Sit opposite the child at a table.

Level 1

1. Beat out a constant rhythm pattern with one of your hands. Have the child look at you and do the same. Don't do more than a two beat rhythm. For example, da-dit, da-dit, da-dit.

Level 2-A

1. Use a two beat rhythm and beat out a constant rhythm pattern with one of your hands. Have him look at you and do the same.

2. Same as #1, but have the child close his eyes and try to match your rhythm pattern.

3. Same as #1 and #2 but use a three beat rhythm, for example, da-dit-dit, da-dit dit.

Level 2-B

1. Beat out a constant rhythm pattern alternating between hands. Child watches you and repeats the rhythm with his hands. For example, R-L-R-L.

2. Do double alterations. For example, R-R-L-L-R-R.

3. Do three alterations. For example, RRR-LLL.

4. Do irregular rhythm. For example, RR-L RR-L. Vary these patterns.

Level 3

1. Beat out a constant rhythm with your hands on the table. Child has his eyes closed. He is to figure out which hands are being used and uses the same hands as he copies the rhythm. Start with double alterations. For example, R-R-L-L-R-R, then three alterations R-R-R-L-L-L, and finally irregular rhythm R-R-R-L-L-R-R.

Level 4

1. This is done with a metronome. The child is to touch his thumb to one of his fingers at the beat of the metronome. Assign numbers to the fingers. (Figure 1) Have him touch the sequence you want to the beat of the metronome. For example, 2,3,4 or 2,4,5.

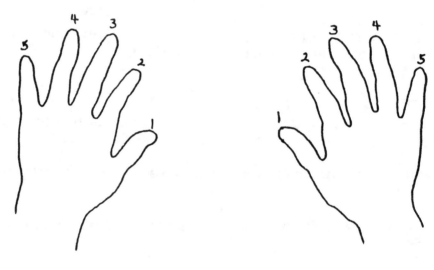

Figure 1

2. Use both hands. For example, 3,2,4 on the right and 3,2,4, on the left.

Level 5

1. This is done with a metronome, with his eyes closed. The child is to touch his thumb to one of his fingers at the beat of the metronome. Assign numbers to his fingers. (Figure 1) Have him touch the sequence you want. For example, 2,3,4,5 or 2,4,5.

2. With his eyes closed alternate hands. For example, 2,4,5 right, 2,5 left.

3. Do 1 and 2 again but with his eyes opened he is to touch the thumb of one hand to the fingers of the other.

Hand Sequencing

Purpose: Sequential Processing

Materials: None

Method: Sit opposite the child at a table. He is to imitate the hand patterns you show him. P means palm down on table, S means side of your hand on table, F means fist on table. Show him a pattern. For example, P.P.S. (palm down, palm down, side of your hand) and he does the same pattern with his hand. For levels 1-4 use only one hand.

Level 1

1. Do two patterns. For example, P.P. or S.P. He then does the same pattern sequence.

Level 2

1. Do three patterns. For example, P.S.P. or F.S.P, or P.P.P. and he does the same pattern sequence.

Level 3

1. Do four patterns. For example, P.P.F.S. or P.S.S.F. and he does the same pattern sequence.

Level 4

1. Do five patterns. For example, P.P.S.S.F. or S.F.F.P.P. and he does the same pattern sequence.

Level 5

1. Do four patterns but alternate hands and he has to use the same hands and in the same sequence you use. For example, right hand P.P. and left hand F.S. or right hand S. F. and left P.S.

SECTION VII

SIMULTANEOUS PROCESSING THERAPY PROCEDURES

Picture Memories

Purpose: Simultaneous Processing

Materials: Magazine pictures

Method: Cut out two pictures from a magazine. Have the child stand in front of the chalkboard and look at an X directly in front of him. Put one picture to the left of the X and the other picture to the right of the X.

Level 1

1. Have the child look at the picture to his left for 10 seconds. Have him close his eyes, count to ten out loud and then with his eyes closed describe as many details of the picture as he can from memory. Do the same with the picture on the right.

Level 2

1. Have the child look at the picture to his left for 10 seconds. Now have him look at the picture to his right and while he is looking at the picture to his right have him describe as many details as he can of the picture to his left. Repeat this by looking at the picture to his left and describing the picture to his right.

New Words

Purpose: Simultaneous Processing

Materials: Newspaper, Instant Words List, Index Cards, Dictionary

Method: Have the child do the following activities:

Level 3

1. Ask the child to read the words from the Instant Words List. (pgs. 219-220) This may be done in more than one session. For each word that the child exhibits difficulty with, make a flash card. Practice the flash cards at each session until the child can identify all of the words.

Level 4

1. Each day have the child find a word in the newspaper that he does not understand. Have the child write down the word. He should also look the word up in a dictionary and write down the definition of the word. Make up flash cards with the words and at the end of each week see how many he can remember. He should be able to pronounce the word, spell it and give you the definition.

Lines and Shapes

Purpose: Simultaneous Processing

Materials: Chalkboard

Method: On a chalkboard, draw a geometric shape (Figure 1) as accurately as you can.

Figure 1

Have four groups of lines for the child to choose from. Ask him which set of lines will make the shape. For example, set "D" in the four groups below makes the shape in figure 1.

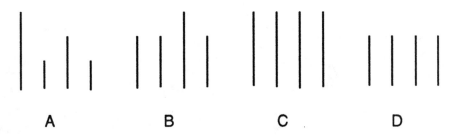

A   B   C   D

Vary the shapes. For example,

Level 2

1. Have the child do the basic shapes as shown above. Think up some new shapes.

Level 3

1. Have the child do the basic shapes but after you show him the shape on the board   hide it from him and make him identify the correct line group from memory.

Level 4

1. Draw the shape on the board, let the child look at it and then hide it from him. Have him identify the correct line group and then draw the shape as accurately as he can on paper.

Visualization

Purpose: Simultaneous Processing

Materials: None

Method: Tell the child we are going to play a game called visualization. It is a pretend game. When we pretend we use our imagination. Here are the rules of the game. Tell the child: 1.) I will tell you about something and ask you to think about it- to imagine and pretend. 2.) Sometimes I will ask you to do something. You must pretend you are doing it. 3.) You are not to speak out. Sit in the chair with your hands on your lap. Close your eyes. You may nod your head "yes" or shake your head "no".

Level 1

1. The following is an example you can use. Make up as many solutions as you can.

   Let's pretend that there is a dish of ice cream on the table in front of you. Do you see it? If yes, shake your head. Pretend to pick up a spoon and eat some of the ice cream. Is it good? Now pretend you are eating the ice cream until it is all gone. When you have finished, pretend to put the spoon back on the table and nod your head yes when you are finished. When the child is finished, have him describe what he pretended to do. For example, what kind of ice cream did he eat? Did it have any whipped cream or cherries on it? etc.

Level 2

1. Same as level 1. Think up as many situations as you can for the child. Unlike level 1, he is to describe the situation out loud. For example, tell him he is in a zoo and have him describe what he sees in his imagination.

Dictionary Training

Purpose: Simultaneous Processing

Materials: Dictionary

Method: Explain to the child how words are located in a dictionary. Once you feel he has an understanding of this, proceed with the activities.

Level 3

1. Each day give the child five words to look up. Time him and record his speed of looking up the words.

Level 4

1. Show the child a word with some of the letters left out. He is to use the dictionary to fill in the spaces. For example, w_r_ . This could be warm, word, etc. Have him find as many words as he can from the dictionary to fill in these spaces.

Letter Position

Purpose: Simultaneous Processing

Materials: Magazine pictures, chalkboard, flash cards, books, colored blocks

Method: The child is to do the following activities.

Level 1

1. Let the child look at a picture from a magazine. As he is looking at it ask him questions about the positions of objects in the picture. For example, the car was next to the tree, the bird was above the house, the man was in front of the lady, etc. If the child is below 6 years old, he will have trouble with his "left and right", therefore, mainly work on concepts such as above, below, in front, behind, etc.

Level 2

1. To make the child aware that position is important, show him a picture from a magazine. Let him look at the picture for five seconds then hide it from him. Ask him if he can remember the positions of certain objects. For example, a car was to the left of a tree, or an airplane was above the house.

Level 3-A

1. The child must understand above and under as well as left and right. Start with geometric shapes and ask him questions about location. For example,

The triangle is above the square number one and square two is to the right of square one. Square one is below the triangle and to the left of square two.

2. Repeat but use letters. For example,   F
   C B

3. Now see if he can do it from memory.

271

Level 3-B

1. Show the child a line of letters. Ask him to remember the positions of certain letters. For example, S,T,O,P,K. The P is to the right of the O and to the left of the K.

Level 3-C

1. Use flash cards with no more than five letters in a row.

   a. Ask him if a certain letter was present or not.

   b. Have him remember and write the letters on the chalkboard.

   c. While his eyes are closed, ask him a letter position. For **example,** what was the third letter from the left?

Level 3-D

1. a. Using a page from a book have him circle common **blends or** common endings.

   b. Find hidden words in words.

Level 4-A

1. With square blocks of different colors make displays. For example,

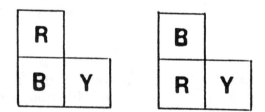

Show him one at a time. From memory he is to build number **one and** number two and tell how they are different. For example, in **#1 R is** above B, in #2 B is above R.

272

Level 4-B

1. Write a letter string on the board. Have him look at it. Ask him to interchange two positions and open his eyes and write the new letter string on the board. For example, A B C D F. Switch the B and C and he should write A C B D F.

Level 4-C

1. On a flash card print several rows of letters. Show the child the card for about 10 seconds. Ask him if a certain letter was present or not. For example, was the letter L present?

Level 5

1. Use the basic sight word list. Write some words on the chalkboard. Ask the child what a word would look like if some of the letters were changed in position. For example, LOST with the O and S interchanged would be LSOT.

Cartoon Pictures

Purpose: Simultaneous Processing

Materials: Cartoons from the newspaper

Method: Cut out a cartoon from the newspaper.   For example, "Peanuts".   Scramble the order of the pictures and see if the child can figure out the proper sequence of action by showing you which picture goes first, second, third, etc. until he shows you the last in the sequence.

Level 3

1. Cut out cartoons from the newspaper or a comic book. Have him put the pictures in the proper sequence.

3-D Tic-Tac-Toe[65]

Purpose: Simultaneous Processing

Materials: Pencil and paper

Method: The child plays Tic-Tac-Toe using three grids at the same time. Draw three tic-tac-toe boxes, lined-up one in front of the other. For example,

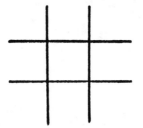

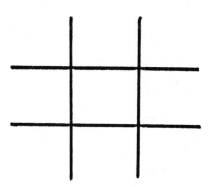

The child thinks of the three grids as being lined up like three light poles, one in front of the other.

Level 4

The child is to play tic-tac-toe using all grids at the same time. For example, he marks an X on the first grid, you mark an O on the second and he marks an X on the third, etc.

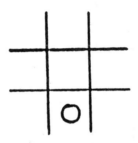

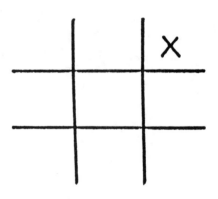

Space Matching

Purpose: Simultaneous Processing

Materials: A length of string, a steel tape or a dressmaker tape

Method: Have the child perform the following tasks. When he has completed each task, measure the distances and compare it to his estimate.

Level 2

1. Ask the child to estimate the number of steps it will take him to walk from where he is standing to some object across the room.

2. Ask him to estimate the number of steps between two objects.

Level 3

1. Ask the child to estimate the distance in feet between two objects.

2. Ask the child to estimate widths, heights, and depths of objects in the room. For example, pictures or window frames.

Level 4

1. Have the child estimate fractional distances between objects. For example, 1/2 or 1/4 the distance between two objects.

Spatial Relationships

Purpose: Simultaneous Processing

Materials: Three colored blocks (The colors used in the activities below are yellow, red, and blue, but any three colors are acceptable.)

Method: Sit opposite the child at a table. Place the three colored blocks in front of him.

Level 1

1. Vary the locations of the blocks and ask the following questions:

   a. Which block is farthest from you?
   b. Which is in the middle?
   c. Which is closest to the blue block?
   d. What color are the blocks on the ends?
   e. Make up various questions concerning the locations of the blocks. Do not stack them on each other.

Level 2

1. Have the child do the following activities with the blocks.

   a. Place the blocks on top of each other so that the yellow is on top and the blue on bottom.
   b. Place them so that the red is higher than the blue, which is higher than the yellow.
   c. Place so the yellow is in front of the red and blue behind the red.
   d. Place so the blue is on top of the yellow and red on top of the blue.
   e. Place so that the blue is lower than the yellow and higher than the red. For example,

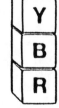

   f. Make up your own variation of the above activities.

Level 3

1. Have the child do the following activities with the blocks.

   a. Place the blocks so the blue is lower than the red yet higher than the yellow. For example,

   b. Place the blocks so the blue is farthest from you with the yellow closest and red in the middle. For example,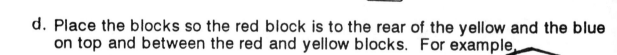

   c. Place the blocks so the red block is beside the yellow and the blue in front of the red. For example,

   d. Place the blocks so the red block is to the rear of the yellow and the blue on top and between the red and yellow blocks. For example,

   e. Make up variations of the above activities.

Orthography Activities

Purpose: Simultaneous Processing

Materials: Dictionary

Method: In English, certain letters occur more frequently in certain positions in words than other letters. This activity is designed to help your child become familiar and pay attention to letter positions in words. For example, in all the english words the letter "T" occurs in the first position more often than any other letter. The following is several lists of letters and their most common position in words. Your child should learn the following lists. They are also used for the activities.

MOST COMMON FIRST LETTER

First most common	- T
Second most common	- A
Third most common	- W
Fourth most common	- H
Fifth most common	- S

MOST COMMON LAST LETTER

First most common	- E
Second most common	- D
Third most common	- T
Fourth most common	- S
Fifth most common	- R

MOST COMMON FIRST TWO LETTERS

First most common	- TH
Second most common	- AN
Third most common	- WA
Fourth most common	- WI
Fifth most common	- HI

MOST COMMON LAST TWO LETTERS

First most common	- HE
Second most common	- ND
Third most common	- AT
Fourth most common	- AS
Fifth most common	- ED

Level 3-A

1. Have your child look up 10 words that start with each of the most common first two letters. List them below:

1.	6.
2.	7.
3.	8.
4.	9.
5.	10.

Level 3-B

1. Have your child look up five words that end with each of the most common last two letters. List them below:

1.

2.

3.

4.

5.

Level 4-A

1. From the newspaper, have your child find as many words as he can with the most common first two letters. Circle the letters. He does not have to write the words down.

Level 4-B

1. From the newspaper, have your child find as many words as he can that end with the most common last two letters. Circle the letters. He does not have to write them down.

Letter Size Spelling

Purpose: Simultaneous Processing

Materials: 5" X 8" index cards

Method: Using lower case letters, make up three large index cards. One card will have all the "short" letters and one card will have all the "tall" letters and one card will have all the "long" letters.

"short" = a,c,e,i,m,n,o,r,s,u,v,w,x,z
"tall" = b,d,f,h,k,l,t
"long" = g,j,p,q,y

An example of letter spelling is as follows:

1. The word "read" would be = short, short, short, tall.

2. The word "pony" would be = long, short, short, long.

3. The word "yard" would be = long, short, short, tall.

Level 3

1. Choose a category such as colors. Ask your child what color is spelled with 3 letters and is spelled short, short, tall? The answer is red.

2. What color is spelled with 4 letters and is tall, tall, short, short? The answer is blue.

3. Continue with other colors.

Level 4

1. Same as Level 3 but use the other categories such as: animals, food, something to drink, etc.

SECTION VIII

VISION THERAPY PROCEDURES

Static Fixation

Purpose: Vision

Materials: None

Method: Have the child do the following activities to improve his fixation skills.

Level 1

1. Have the child lie on his back with his head up. Mark a spot high on the wall for him to look at. Stand over the child and pull him to a sitting position. The child should never take his eyes off the spot on the wall.

2. Have the child sit and rock back and forth without taking his eyes off the spot on the wall.

3. As the child is standing, have him walk around and not take his eyes off the spot on the wall.

4. As the child is standing and looking at the spot on the wall, have him jump completely around and pick up a spot on the opposite wall.

Pencil Push Ups

Purpose: Vision

Materials: Pencil

Method: This activity trains a child's eye teaming skills. Watch the child's eyes and make a note at what distance one of his eyes stops looking at the pencil and drifts outward.

Level 2

1. Have the child seated in a chair and holding a pencil in one of his hands at arm's length. Have him slowly move the pencil in towards his nose. Make sure he moves the pencil slowly. See how close he can move it before he sees double (two pencils) or you see one of his eyes turn outward. Force the child to keep his eyes on the top of the pencil. The goal is to have the child move the pencil all the way into his nose. Each day make a note as to how close he got it to his nose.

Brock String

Purpose: Vision

Materials: Brockstring, metronome

Method: Level 2 is done with a 3 foot length of rough textured string with three large sized colored beads. Level 3 is done with an 18 inch length of string between two tongue depressors. Drill a hole near the top of the tongue depressors and put three small colored beads on the string. Tie a knot on the outside of the tongue depressors. For example,

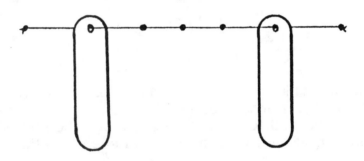

Level 2

1. Tie one end of the string to the top of a chair. The child holds the other end taut against his nose. At your command or at the beat of a metronome he looks from one bead to the other quickly and accurately. Vary the locations of the beads on the string. Don't put the first bead closer than five inches from the child's nose. Have him call the color of the beads as he moves his eyes from one bead to the other. For example,

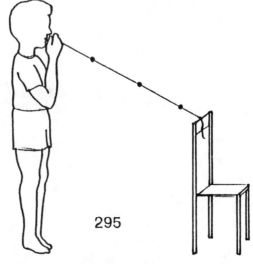

295

Level 3

1. The child holds one tongue depressor at his nose and the other is held away from his face so that the string is taut. At your command, the child moves his eyes quickly and accurately from one bead to another. You may vary the distance and locations of the beads on the string. Don't have the first bead closer than 4 inches from his nose. For example,

2. Have the child do the same as #1 but have him hold the end that is away from his nose in different positions. For example, down and to the right or up and to the left. As you use the metronome, have him move his eyes quickly from bead to bead each time the metronome beats.

Push Up Amp

Purpose: Vision

Materials: Small book print

Method: This activity is done with only one eye at a time. (have the child cover his other eye) When he can do it easily with each of his eyes, then have him do it with both of his eyes together. If the child has difficulty with the size print, use a larger size print and work down to the smaller size.

Level 2

1. Have the child seated. Hold the printed material at 16" in front of his eye. Ask him if the print is clear. If it is, slowly move the print in towards his eye. He is to tell you when the print starts to blur. When it starts to blur, have him try to force himself to make the print clear. If he can clear it, move the card closer to his eye. When you reach the point where the child cannot get the print clear after a few seconds, move the card away from him and start over. Don't move the card closer than four inches from his eye.

Baseball Fixations

Purpose: Vision

Materials: Blackboard

Method: Have the child stand about five feet in front of the board. Draw an X at his eye level. Draw four numbers randomly around the board. For example,

2

3   **x**

        4

1

Level 2

1. a. Stand facing the child so you can watch his eyes but not block his view of the numbers on the board.

   b. The child starts by looking at an "X" directly in front of him drawn on the board. He is to look at the "X" but be aware of the other numbers drawn around it. He is not to move his head or take his eyes off of the "X".

   c. You call out one of the numbers. The child is to move his eyes to that number quickly and accurately. If he does this without looking at any of the other numbers, you give him credit for a hit and he gets to first base.

   d. Watch his eyes, if he takes his eyes off of the number or looks at you, you call him out.

   e. Call out another number. The child now moves his eyes quickly and accurately to that number. If he does it without looking at another number, you give him credit and he gets to second base.

   f. You continue to watch his eyes. If he takes his eyes off of the number he is supposed to be looking at, call him out.

299

g. He is to try and get all the way home (this would be four numbers) without getting three outs. You can call the numbers in any random order. You can also use letters instead of numbers.

h. Remember an "out" occurs if he does not look directly at the number you call or if he takes his eyes off of that number before you call the next one.

Peripheral Training

Purpose: Vision

Materials: Span of recognition worksheets, clear plastic sheet with letters

Method: These activities train peripheral awareness. Peripheral awareness should be stressed with every activity that you do. Always make the child aware of his peripheral vision. In all of these activities the child should keep his head and eyes straight ahead.

Level 1

1. Stand next to the child and have him stare straight ahead. Hold a familiar object in your hand. For example, a pencil, set of keys, etc. Slowly move it into his field of vision until he can recognize it.

Level 2

1. Print a word on a flash card. Slowly move it into his field of vision from the side until he recognizes the word.

2. Print a word on a flash card. Hold it at his side until he can just start to see it. Ask him to guess how many letters are in the word. Ask him what the first letter is.

Level 3

1. Open a book and have him put his finger on the middle of the page. As he looks at his finger, ask him to see how far to the left and right he can recognize words or letters. The average person should be able to identify at least two letters to the left of the fixation point and four or five on the right.

Level 4

1. Get a transparency about the size of a sheet of notebook paper. Put a dot in the center and cut out letters of various sizes to paste in various locations around the center dot. Hold the plastic in front of him so that you are looking directly through it at his eyes. Tell him to find and point to certain letters without moving his eyes off of the center dot.   Once he can do the entire alphabet then have him find letter combinations that spell out words. Hold the plastic about 16 inches in front of the child.

2. Use the span of recognition sheets. (Figures 1,2,3,) Start with sheet number one.   Have the child stare at the X and tell how many numbers he can see on the left and right of the X. Do sheets two and three next. Make sure he does not move his eyes off of the X. He is only to use his peripheral vision to see the numbers on the side of the X.

Figure 1. **SPAN OF RECOGNITION 1**

7320X2549	4832X8754
9508X3026	7203X8402
8674X0463	065X7013
3658X2093	1057X2015
9579X4802	1098X4597
3645X8012	3048X9734
4026X3489	5830X8754
7468X1804	1574X0196
2435X9087	8543X8590
7539X1912	2904X1568
1048X6371	4872X9156
4845X9501	3807X5739
6842X5608	1498X6903
2465X1065	9375X0289
3208X4960	3412X5321
2032X8756	087X1870
1085X7601	4182X2308
1208X6730	6907X4638
9804X1645	4902X1497
1760X4973	1258X9168
4065X1357	1420X1754
3058X7940	1760X7532

Figure 2. **SPAN OF RECOGNITION 2**

8032 X 6408	8046 X 2308
8146 X 7145	1024 X 4512
1921 X 7539	2084 X 3902
7849 X 4502	6804 X 4068
3860 X 2076	1024 X 8901
4976 X 9794	5648 X 2012
3783 X 9701	7019 X 3852
7102 X 4856	8046 X 0342
1574 X 5982	9013 X 2304
6790 X 1426	3468 X 8421
1036 X 9753	8651 X 3012
9702 X 7407	7654 X 3718
3862 X 7390	7031 X 2987
9074 X 4574	3857 X 9482
3802 X 5015	8352 X 2476
8765 X 6842	2450 X 8632
8042 X 2671	4321 X 8704
3571 X 0932	6453 X 2467
0421 X 7654	9061 X 7430
7321 X 8613	1324 X 2814
8214 X 9462	6502 X 5301
0145 X 8734	2131 X 0141

Figure 3. SPAN OF RECOGNITION 3

8759	X	4302		2103	X	6517
2867	X	3402		4902	X	1415
3210	X	3890		1617	X	8010
4902	X	8634		5021	X	0932
0214	X	3905		8472	X	9012
9135	X	2356		0648	X	1045
1047	X	2487		1243	X	2482
1032	X	2913		2163	X	4010
2450	X	1456		6830	X	1912
1041	X	1312		0249	X	6502
4078	X	5890		5863	X	2059
3158	X	6820		1375	X	0492
4921	X	0132		9068	X	3187
6132	X	9856		8146	X	4902
1065	X	2486		1516	X	9101
1097	X	1505		4182	X	4081
3922	X	4721		5976	X	3521
0156	X	3803		0428	X	7632
9568	X	1715		2860	X	5073
2191	X	6804		6721	X	7342
5032	X	2139		1056	X	6503
8072	X	6408		4892	X	0738

Example of A Daily Activities Sheet

Date	Activity	Time	Observations
6-1-90	Walking Rail Level 2-A	10 min.	Having a lot of difficulty with his balance
6-1-90	Bean Bag Level 2	10 min.	Much better than yesterday
6-1-90	Rhythm Level 2-A	5 min.	Very difficult - do this exercise again at a later date
6-1-90	Bilateral Circles Level 2	10 min.	Some difficulty keeping up with his left hand
6-1-90	Pencil Push Ups Level 2	5 min.	Got to within 8 inches of his nose

Example of A Daily Activities Sheet

Date	Activity	Time	Observations
6-3-90	Walking Rail Level 2-A	10 min.	Balance is better today but need to continue working with this one
6-3-90	Gross Motor Sequence Level 2	5 min.	This exercise seems very beneficial - continue it next time
6-3-90	Numbered Circles on Blackboard Level 2	5 min.	Having a lot of difficulty with this - needs more work with it
6-3-90	Pencils With Numbers Level 2	5 min.	Had to remind him not to move his head
6-3-90	Bilateral Circles Level 2	10 min.	Still had problems with his left hand - practice with just his left hand

Daily Activities Sheet

Date	Activity	Time	Observations

Daily Activities Sheet

Date	Activity	Time	Observations

Daily Activities Sheet

Date	Activity	Time	Observations

Daily Activities Sheet

Date	Activity	Time	Observations

Daily Activities Sheet

Date	Activity	Time	Observations

Daily Activities Sheet

Date	Activity	Time	Observations

Daily Activities Sheet

Date	Activity	Time	Observations

Daily Activities Sheet

Date	Activity	Time	Observations

MATERIALS AND EQUIPMENT LIST

The following is a list of the materials and equipment that you will need to do the activities in this book. A one (1) indicates that it comes with this book. A two (2) indicates that you will be given instructions either in the glossary or with the activity on how to make it.

1. Chalkboard
2. Colored Chalk
3. Colored Pens
4. Metronome
5. Walking Rail (2)
6. Small Trampoline
7. Balance Board (2)
8. Playground Ball
9. Marsden Ball (2)
10. Masking Tape (plain and colored)
11. Colored Tile or Carpet Squares
12. Clothespins (the type you pinch)
13. 7' Jump Rope
14. Bean Bags
15. Various Sized Nuts and Bolts
16. Pint Size Jar Filled with Dried Lima Beans
17. Fixation Chart (Letter Chart) (1)
18. Decode Chart (1)
19. Two Flashlights
20. Pen Light
21. Protractor
22. Measuring Tape
23. Colored Blocks
24. 7" x 10" Mirror
25. Rubber Bands
26. V.M.C. Bat (2)
27. Wooden Yardstick
28. Colored Pins
29. Brockstring (2)
30. Span of Recognition Worksheets (1)

31. Visual Motor Activity Chart (1)
32. Directional Arrows Chart (1)
33. Directional "U" Worksheet (1)
34. b-d-p-q Worksheet

REFERENCES

1. Association for Children and Adults with Learning Disabilities. 4156 Library Rd, Pittsburg, PA., 15234.

2. Swindoll, Charles R. "Come Before Winter." Multnomah Press. Portland, Oregon. 1985.

3. Frostig, Marianne., Ph.D. "Perceptual Training, The State of the Art." COVD. Paper Number 182938. 1978.

4. Ayres, Jean A., Ph.D. "Sensory Integration and Learning Disorders." Western Psychological Services. 1978, p. 15.

5. Frankenburg, William K., M.D. and Dodds, Josiah B., Ph.D. "Denver Developmental Screening Test." University of Colorado Medical Center.

6. Ibid.

7. Beery, Keith E. "Revised Administration, Scoring, and Teaching Manual for the Developmental Test of Visual-Motor Integration." Modern Curriculum Press. 1982.

8. DeQuiros, Julio B., M.D., Ph.D., and Schrager, Orlando L., M.D. "Neuropsychological Fundamentals in Learning Disabilities." Academic Therapy Publications. Novato, CA. 1979, p. 39.

9. Corballis, Michael C., and Beale, Ivan L. "The Ambivalent Mind." Nelson-Hall. Chicago, IL. 1983, p. 187.

10. Crosby, R.M.N., M.D. with Liston, Robert A. "The Waysiders: Reading and the Dyslexic Child." The John Day Company. New York. 1976, pp. 13, 54, 3.

11. Pirozzolo, Francis J. and Wittrock, Merlin C. "Neuropsychological and Cognitive Processes in Reading." Academic Press. 1981, p. 146.

12. Sinatra, Richard. "Fixations, Memory, and Implications for Classroom Reading Instruction." COVD. Paper Number 167956. September 1978.

13. McConkie, George, and Others. "Toward the Use of Eye Movements in the Study of Language Processing. Technical Report No. 134." COVD. Paper Number 174968. August 1979.

14. Elsendoorn, Ben A.G. and Bouma, Herman. "Working Models of Human Perception." Academic Press. 1989, p. 277.

15. Wolverton, Gary S. "The Acquisition of Visual Information During Fixations and Saccades in Reading." COVD. Paper Number 178861. April 1979.

16. Rayner, Keith. "Eye Movements in Reading." Academic Press. 1983, p. 116.

17. Gosnell, Robert G., O.D. "Deficits of Temporal Processing in Higher Visual Perception: "A Cause of Specific Reading Disabilities?" O.E.P. Curriculum II, Volume 61, Number 9, June 1989.

18. Elsendoorn, p. 294.

19. Pirozzolo, p. 178.

20. Ibid., p. 180.

21. Ibid., p. 171.

22. Henderson, Leslie. "Orthography and Word Recognition in Reading." Academic Press. 1982, p. 283.

23. Haber, Ralph Norman. "How We Remember What We See." Scientific American. May 1970, Volume 222, Number 5.

24. Pribram, Karl H. "Languages of the Brain." Prentice-Hall, Inc. 1971.

25. Prith, Uta. and Vogel, Juliet M. "Grammar of Two Dimensional Space and Getting Letters Straight", Paper presented at The International Reading Association, Newark, DE. Available from International Reading Association. 800 Barksdale Rd., P.O. Box 8139, Newark, DE., 19711.

26. Shapero, Max, B.S., O.D., Cline, David, B.S. and Hofstetter, Henry W., B.S., M.S., Ph.D. "Dictionary of Visual Science." Chilton Book Company. 1968, Second Edition.

27. Elsendoorn, p. 270

28. Pirozzolo, p. 170.

29. Henderson, p. 289.

30. Treisman, Anne. and Gormican, Stephen. "Feature Analysis in Early Vision: Evidence from Search Asymmetries." Psychological Review. 1988, Vol. 95, No. 1, p. 15-48.

31. Mayzner, M.S. and Tresselt, M.E. "Tables of Single-Letter and Diagram Frequency Counts for Various Word-Length and Letter-Position Combinations." Psychonomic Press. 1965, Vol. 1, No. 2.

32. Wicklund, David A. and Katz, Leonard. "Perception and Retention in Children's Reading." COVD. Paper Number 160981, Connecticut University, Department of Psychology, 1977.

33. Morris, Helen F. "Manual for the EDL/Biometrics Reading Eye II." McGraw-Hill, Inc. 1973.

34. Fantz, Robert L. "The Origin of Form Peception." Perception: Mechanisms and Models. W.H. Freeman and Company. 1972, p. 334. .

35. Dougan-Serex, Diane., O.D. "Infant Vision." Optometric Extension Program Foundation. 1988, Series 1, No, 2.

36. Bower, T.G.R. "The Object in the World of the Infant." Scientific American. Oct. 1971, Vol. 225, No. 4, pp. 30-38.

37. Bower, T.G.R. "The Visual World of Infants." Perception: Mechanisms and Models. W.H. Freeman and Company. 1972, p. 356.

38. Fantz, p. 337.

39. Ayres, Chapter 12.

40. Frostig, Marianne., Ph.D. "Perceptual Training, The State of the Art." COVD. Paper Number 182938. Frostig.

41. DeQuiros, p. 86.

42. Ibid., p. 60.

43. Dover, William., O.D. "Developmental Motor Responses by Age." Journal of Optometric Vision Development. December 1979, Volume 10, Number 4.

44. DeQuiros, p. 78

45. Ayres, p. 17

46. Ibid., p. 8.

47. DeQuiros, p. 70.

48. Levinson, Harold N., M.D. "Dyslexia: A Solution to the Riddle." Springer-Velag, Inc. New York. 1980.

49. Ayres, p. 46.

50. Ibid., p. 4.

51. DeQuiros, p. 30.

52. Ibid., p. 50.

53. Ibid., p. 67.

54. Ginsburg, Oppers H. "Piaget's Theory of Intellectual Development." Prentice-Hall, Inc. New York. 1969.

55. Kephart, Newell C. "The Slow Learner in the Classroom." Charles E. Merrill Books, Inc. 1960, p. 21.

56. Wold, Robert M. "Visual and Perceptual Aspects for the Achieving and Underachieving Child." Special Child Publications, Inc. 1969. p. 47

57. Kaufman, Alan S. and Kaufman, Nadeen L. "Kaufman Assessment Battery for Children. Interpretive Manual." American Guidance Service, Inc. 1983.

58. Ibid.

59. Schatzow, Margaret., Ph.D. "Sensory Integration, Cognitive Development and School Achievement." O.E.P., Curriculum II. July 1989.

60. Prith, Uta and Vogel, Juliet M. "Grammar of Two Dimensional Space and Getting Letters Straight." Paper presented at the International Reading Association, Newark, DE. Available from International Reading Association, 800 Barksdale Rd., P.O. Box 8139, Newark, DE., 19711. Prith.

61. Kephart, pp. 43-44

62. Strauss, Robert N. and DeOreo, Karen. "Assessment of Individual Motor Skills." Activities Manual. Education Service Center, 7703 North Lamar Blvd., Austin, Texas 78752. p. 143.

63. Ibid., p. 214-217.

64. Kirshner, A.J. "Training That Makes Sense." Academic Therapy Publications. Novato, California. 1972, pp. 62-63.

65. Richards, Regina G., M.A. "Classroom Visual Activities." Academic Therapy Publications. Novato, California. 1988, p. 65.

66. Strauss, pp. 188-192.

67. Lane, Kenneth A., O.D. "Reversal Errors Theories and Therapy Procedures." Vision Extension. Santa Ana, California. 1988, p. 17.

68. Ibid., p. 21.

69. Ibid., p. 27.

70. Ibid., p. 31.

71. Ibid., p. 67.

72. Ibid., p. 71.

73. Ibid., p. 83.

74. Ibid., p. 91.

75. Ibid., p. 131.

76. Fry, Edward B., Ph.D. "Instant Words." Fountoukidis, Dona & Polk, Jaqueline. "The New Reading Teachers Book of Lists." Prentice Hall, Englewood Cliffs, New Jersey. 1985.

GLOSSARY OF TERMS

Balance Board - A square or round board about two and one-half feet in diameter. The board is balanced on a piece of wood about six inches in diameter and tapered to about three inches. The child stands on the board to improve his balance skills.

Brain Stem - The stemlike portion of the brain connecting the cerebral hemispheres with the spinal cord.

Cerebellum - A part of the brain that occupies the posterior cranial fossa behind the brain stem. It is concerned with the coordination of movements, especially eye-hand coordination and eye movements.

Cerebral Cortex - The thin layer of gray matter on the surface of the cerebral hemisphere. It is responsible for our higher mental functions including reading and perception.

Cognitive Processing - Includes all aspects of perceiving, thinking, and remembering.

Context Clues - Help us understand what we are reading as a result of being familiar with the topic or theme we are reading about.

Corporal Potentiality - Excluding bodily interference in order to obtain higher learning processes.

Cortical - Same as cerebral cortex.

Directionality - Understanding an external object's proper orientation. (ie, the proper orientation of letters and numbers)

Feature Detectors - Are located in the fovea and are probably the cones. They are used to discriminate the different features of letters for letter and word identification.

Fine Motor - Refers to activities that require small muscle movements. (ie, eye movements, writing, etc.)

Fixation - The act of directing the eyes to the object we are looking at so that the image of the object can be centered on the fovea.

Fixation Chart - A chart with rows of numbers on it.

Fixation Point - The object of which the eyes are directed to during a fixation. (ie, a letter in a word)

Fovea - The small 1 1/2 mm area of the retina where the cones are located. This is the area of the retina where we get our color vision and sharp visual acuity. Light must focus on this area for clear vision.

Gross Motor - Refers to activities that require large muscle movements. (ie, walking, balancing, hopping, etc.)

Laterality - The internal awareness of the two sides of the body and their differences. For a child, this is his ability to know his right side from his left.

Letter Chart - A chart with rows of letters on it.

Marsden Ball - A ball, two to three inches in diameter, hung from the ceiling by a string. It is used in many motor and vision training procedures.

Metronome - An instrument for beating a desired time. It is used as an aid in practicing music.

Motor Skills - Includes both gross and fine motor skills.

Ocular Motor - Pertains to movements of the eyes, especially movements involved in following a moving object.

Orthography - Spelling patterns. The art of understanding the proper positions of letters in words.

Perception - Recognition and identification of our environment. Visual perception would be visual recognition and identification of our environment.

Perceptual Motor - Refers to perceptual and motor skills. Perceptual development is accomplished through motor involvement.

Peripheral Vision - Refers to vision other than central vision. As we look at an object, the area to the side of what we are looking at is in our peripheral vision.

Regression - Indicates rereading. Any time the eye moves back to the left instead of the right as we read across a page.

Saccadic Eye Movements - Rapid, accurate eye movement from fixation point to fixation point.

Semantics - Knowledge of word meaning.

Sequential Processing - The ability to process information given to you a little at a time in consecutive order. Children who have problems in sequential processing have difficulty remembering things in sequence. (ie, the letters in the alphabet or lists of spelling words)

Simultaneous Processing - The ability to process many pieces of information given to you all at once. Children who have simultaneous processing problems may have poor reading comprehension skills.

Span of Recognition - The amount of print that the brain can recognize during a single fixation.

Sustained Activity - The neurological activity that processes the visual information of the letters and words we are looking at.

Syntax - Knowledge of grammar and word associations to make sense of a sentence.

Transient Channels - A short duration response that shuts off the visual processing of the sustained system. It is triggered by our eye movement when we move our eyes from fixation point to fixation point during reading.

Vestibular System - The non-auditory organs of the inner ear dedicated to posture, equilibrium, balance, muscular tones, and orientation in environmental space.

Vision - Includes not only seeing the 20/20 line of print but all visual skills including focusing, eye teaming, and eye tracking.

Visual Motor - Pertains to eye-hand coordination skills. (ie, the ability to copy and reproduce a geometric shape or letter accurately)

V.M.C. Bat (Visual Motor Control Bat) - This is a dowel rod about three feet long and one inch in diameter. It is divided into colored sections and is used for gross motor and eye-hand coordination activities.

Visual Persistence - Refers to the continued processing of visual information from the previous fixation. It is usually the result of not having the transient channels functioning properly.

Walking Rail - A six to eight foot long (2" x 4") board that is balanced on three (4" x 4") sections. It is used for balance and gross motor activities.

INDEX

A

Abstract Written Code, 5
Auditory Perception, 10
Automatic Levels, 12

B

Balance, 12, 13, 16
Balance Board, 37, 49, 137, 203, 327
Balance Disc, see Balance Board
Bean Bag, 67
Blackboard, 87, 93, 95, 107, 117, 121, 123,
            133, 151, 161, 171, 183, 185,
            187, 201, 215, 225, 227, 229,
            235, 239, 241, 243, 247, 265,
            271, 299
Body Schemes, 10
Brain Stem, 11, 12, 327
Brockstring, 295

C

Central Nervous System, 12, 13
Central Vision, 5, 13
Cerebellum, 11, 327
Cerebellum - Vestibular, 13
Cerebral Cortex, 11, 12, 327
Chalkboard, see Blackboard
Cognitive Processing, 4, 327
Cognitive Skills, 11

Completion, 10
Context Clues, 4, 5, 327
Contextual Information, 3
Corporal Potentiality, 12, 327
Cortex, see Cerebral Cortex
Crowding, 6

D

Decode Chart, 153
Developmental Sequence, 10
Directional Arrows Work Sheet, 211
Directional "U" Work Sheet, 209
Directionality, 16, 17, 327
Directionality Activities, 201-243
Distractability, 12

E

Equilibrium, 11
Eye Hand Coordination, 13
Eye Movements, 12
Eye Tracking Skills, 13

F

Fast And Slow Processes, 4
Feature Detectors, 6, 7, 327
Feature Identification, 7
Fine Motor Skills, 2, 7, 13, 328

Regressions, 3, 329
Retina, 13
Right And Left, 2, 13, 16
Reversing, 2, 6
Rods, 6

S

Saccadic Eye Movement, 3, 4, 329
Saccadic Fixation, 4
Saccadic Suppression, 4
Saccule, 11
Salient Feature, 6
Scan Pattern, 6
Self Reference System, 16
Semantic Clues, 4, 5, 7, 329
Semantic Relationships, 15
Semicircular Canals, 11
Sensory Stimuli, 10
Sequential Processing, 15, 17, 18, 329
Sequential Processing Activities, 247-257
Simultaneous Processing, 15, 17, 329
Simultaneous Processing Activities, 261-287
Size Consistency, 10
Span Of Recognition, 3, 329
Spatial Orientation, 11
Speech Development, 2
Stroke Sequence Chart, 103
Sustained Activity, 4, 329
Syntaxic Clues, 4, 5, 7, 329

T

Tactile Percpetion, 10
Trampoline, 41
Transient Channels, 4, 329

U

Utricle, 11

V

Verbal Instructions, 15
Vestibular Influences, 10
Vestibular System, 11, 329
Vision, 13, 14, 16, 17, 329
Vision Activities, 291-309
Vision Perception, 10
Visual Acuity, 4, 9
Visual Image, 3
Visual Information, 3
Visual Motor, 13, 17, 18, 329
Visual Motor Activities, 81-117
Visual Motor Activity Sheet, 189
Visual Persistence, 4, 329
Visual Skills, 7
Visual Stimuli, 10
Voluntary Motor Activities, 12
V.M.C. Bat, 37, 125, 329

W

Walking Rail, 57, 137, 203, 330

ABOUT
THE AUTHOR

Dr. Kenneth A. Lane is a Developmental Optometrist who is well known for his work with children who have learning problems. A strong believer in multiprofessional help for children, Dr. Lane founded the Lewisville Learning Clinic in 1980. He has lectured extensively to parents, teachers and optometrists and has had several articles published in professional journals. Dr. Lane's first book, Reversal Errors: Theories and Therapy Procedures, was published in 1988. Developing Your Child for Success is the result of ten years of experience of working with and helping children overcome their learning disabilities.

Order Form For
DEVELOPING YOUR CHILD FOR SUCCESS
by Dr. Kenneth A. Lane, O.D.

Mail to: Learning Potentials Publishers, Inc.
          230 West Main Street
          Lewisville, Texas 75057

Yes . . . please send me _____ copies of **Developing Your Child For Success** at $24.95.
(Please print or type)

NAME:_____ PHONE: _____

COMPANY:_____

ADDRESS: _____

CITY:_____ STATE: _____ ZIP: _____

_____ I have enclosed my check or money order for **Developing Your Child For Success.**
Please add $3.00 per book for postage and handling. Texas residents include 7.25%
($1.81 per book) state sales tax. (Orders from outside the United States must be
accommpanied by a postal money order in U.S. funds). Allow 30 days for delivery.

_____ Please bill me.

Quantity orders invited. For bulk discount prices, please call:
(214)-221-2564

Developing Your Child For Success
Seminar And Workshop

Target Audiences

*Parents, Optometrists, Teachers, Occupational Therapists,
Diagnosticians, Principals, Therapists*

This seminar is designed to give a better understanding of the complex
processes involved in reading. It will explain how visual and motor skills are
critical for visual perceptual development. It will increase awareness of the
perceptual skills that young children need to succeed in school.

The workshop will explain some of the activities in **Developing Your Child For
Success** and train those who are interested in how to effectively use these
activities.

For seminar and workshop information, please call (214) 221-2564.